THE STRATEGIC STORYTELLER

THE STRATEGIC STORYTELLER

CONTENT MARKETING IN THE AGE OF THE EDUCATED CONSUMER

ALEXANDER JUTKOWITZ

WILEY

Published by John Wiley & Sons, Inc., Hoboken, New Jersey
Published simultaneously in Canada

For general information about our other products and services, please contact our Customer Care Department within the United States at (800) 762-2974, outside the United States at (317) 572-3993 or fax (317) 572-4002.

Wiley publishes in a variety of print and electronic formats and by print-on-demand. Some material included with standard print versions of this book may not be included in e-books or in print-on-demand. If this book refers to media such as a CD or DVD that is not included in the version you purchased, you may download this material at http://booksupport.wiley.com. For more information about Wiley products, visit www.wiley.com.

Library of Congress Cataloging-in-Publication Data

Names: Jutkowitz, Alexander, 1968– author.
Title: The strategic storyteller : content marketing in the age of the
    educated consumer / Alexander Jutkowitz.
Description: Hoboken, New Jersey : John Wiley & Sons, Inc., [2017] |
Identifiers: LCCN 2017020141 (print) | LCCN 2017032080 (ebook) |
    ISBN 9781119351443 (pdf) | ISBN 9781119345091 (epub) |
    ISBN 9781119345114 (cloth)
Subjects: LCSH: Marketing. | Storytelling. | Content (Psychology)
Classification: LCC HF5415 (ebook) | LCC HF5415 .J87 2017 (print) |
    DDC 658.8/02—dc23
LC record available at https://lccn.loc.gov/2017020141

Cover Design: Wiley
Cover Illustration: © Group SJR

Printed in the United States of America

10 9 8 7 6 5 4 3 2 1

To Ali and Teddy, my bunny and bear.

Contents

Introduction: A Call for Storytellers

If we cannot tell a story about what happened to us, nothing has happened to us.

—James P. Carse

The world is in dire need of stories. Information is abundant, but stories are rare.

It is not a subjective impression that our lives are getting faster and more complex. We are speaking faster than we were a decade ago, perhaps because we have more to say given that the amount of data in the world is growing at a rate of 60 percent per year.

In response, organizations have grown 35 times more complex over the past seven decades. For those of us who live our lives inside organizations, lead them, or communicate for them, this means that our day-to-day experience is ever tougher to manage.

As if this were not enough, the stories we get about the world are not in agreement with one another. Open the pages of any major news outlet, and you will find stories of precarious societies riven by violence, ideological conflict, and environmental collapse. Yet against this continuous buzz of catastrophe, it is also somehow true that the share of the global population living in extreme poverty has fallen by 50 percent since 1990. Which story to believe? And if both are to be believed, what larger story can explain them both?

If we're going to make sense of all this, we need more storytellers. We need more people with the tools and the desire to dig into the world's information and build their own stories out of it.

As digital technology breaks down the barriers between jobs, sooner or later all of us will be asked to tell stories in the course of our professional lives. We will be asked to make a case for ourselves, our work, our companies, and our future.

This is good news, because when we tell stories, unique and useful things happen.

Storytelling flexes the same muscles that allow organizations to pivot quickly around crisis or opportunity. To construct a coherent story requires that we make connections between parts of ourselves and our companies that wouldn't otherwise exist. Having these connections ready can mean the difference between survival or failure when we are met by the inevitable shocks of the future.

Innovation and creativity are the defining words of this collective moment. Key to both is the ability to take whatever raw materials are in front of us and recombine them in new ways. These raw materials can be ideas, physical assets, parts of organizations, and the talents of the people who work for them. And when we tell stories about ourselves and our institutions, we have no choice but to learn everything we can about these raw materials, and often we have to go in search of new ones. The raw materials that make up the solutions to our toughest problems are a kind of useful industrial by-product of the storytelling process.

Storytelling is also an inherently disruptive activity.

On a personal level, it means that strategic storytellers must expand their capabilities and learn to think in new ways. In the course of telling a story, they might wear the hat of a consultant, artist, detective, journalist, or executive.

On an organizational level, storytelling requires us to find new language and images to represent our goals and our purpose that can be understood by a wider audience, not just the small circles that already speak our jargon. By making our purpose clear to others, we make it clear to ourselves.

On a strategic level, a fully grown storytelling function within an organization can mean the difference between life and death. Stories are the lifeblood of political campaigns. In the history of U.S. politics, it's the figures with the best stories that also radiate the most power, even generations after their deaths. We all know a few anecdotes or have a general sense of the personal brand of our greatest presidents, like Washington, Lincoln, and Teddy Roosevelt. In contemporary politics, the right story can win or lose an election, pass a piece of legislation, or end a war. In business, the right story defines any company's most valuable asset: its brand.

Stories are the base unit of reputation. Not to tell your own is to have no reputation or to cede its construction to others.

And that's where this book comes in. In it are the tools to build stories in a new way that coexists with the accelerated, complex tempo of our lives.

Our most important stories don't just live in the static pages of books any more. They are shaped and told digitally, at high speed, and emerge just a half step behind experience. They are consumed and made in small windows of time and in little sips of attention.

It is my firm belief that these conditions do not lessen our stories—but only make them richer. In fact, the rapid pace and diffusion of our stories—what I call their velocity and atomization—are making storytelling a lot more fun.

In that spirit, what you'll find in this book does not need to be consumed in order—or even in its entirety—to be useful. It's my hope that you can dip into this book at any spot for a bit of inspiration or for your next urgently needed idea.

When you need to be a storyteller any page of this book, consumed in whatever niche of time you might have, is here to help.

So let's advance to the next the page (whether digital or analog) and find not just my story but the beginning of yours, too.

THE STRATEGIC
STORYTELLER

Wisdom, Wonder, and Delight

Glamour and Grammar

The career of every revolutionary ends in glamour.

I don't mean the superficial definition of glamour, an artificial sense of beauty that props up a celebrity. I am talking about its deeper meaning, which is related to the stories we tell. The word *glamour* literally means a magic spell created by language. To be "beglamoured" means to be enchanted. Glamour was coined long ago as a mispronunciation of "grammar," because writing—with its power to put lasting ideas directly into people's heads without speech—seemed like magic to those who had never seen it before.

This kind of magic is still potent. You can see it in the stories we tell about political figures, especially the ones who changed history.

The journey of Mahatma Gandhi, the revolutionary who peacefully liberated India from the British Empire in the early twentieth century, began in a deserted railway station one lonely night after he found himself kicked out of a train compartment. Even though Gandhi was a lawyer and could afford a first-class ticket, he was excluded from riding in the carriage because of his brown skin. Starting with that moment of powerlessness, Gandhi began to transform his life and then the life of his entire nation. Over the next few decades until his death, he would build a movement that ended white, apartheid rule in India.

But Gandhi's journey didn't end with his eventual assassination. It continues through his existence as a lasting icon of progress and change. His image has been used to bolster the power of modern governments, and it's also been used to sell computers in the United States. In the 1990s, Apple featured him in one of their first "Think Different" ads.

The glamour of another revolutionary, Alexander Hamilton, is currently selling record numbers of tickets on Broadway to the musical about Hamilton's life written by Lin-Manuel Miranda. As of this writing, Hamilton's glamour is worth about $1.9 million per week in ticket sales.

Another American revolutionary, Benjamin Franklin, recognized the power of his own glamour while he was still alive. To get attention and enhance his influence in Paris, where he was stationed as the first U.S. ambassador, he exaggerated his own persona by wearing a coonskin fur cap. Franklin had worn the cap out of necessity on the long voyage from the United States to France to keep his bald head warm. But to French high society, such a primitive piece of clothing wasn't a necessity but a charming symbol of American ruggedness.

I first learned about the glamour of revolutionaries and the power of their images at an early age. When I was a boy in Chile my parents told me to rip up my Fidel Castro poster on the day that Augusto Pinochet came to power. Castro was a communist and Pinochet was a fascist, so Pinochet hated everything Castro stood for. Even though the poster was on the wall of my bedroom in the privacy of our home, my parents told me it had to come down. So that day I learned that a piece of paper with an image and words had enough symbolic power that it could somehow be a threat to people who held real political power. To my childhood self, it seemed like magic.

I also learned that, whether in pixels or print, stories take up physical space in our lives. Once created and let loose into the world, the content that a story takes shape in becomes a conduit for influence and power.

I suppose one of the reasons I chose to pursue a career as a pollster and political strategist was to follow those conduits of influence to their origins, to figure out how the magic worked. I was always sure that hiding in the reams of data I gathered on voters, there was an overarching story about whatever country I was working in. Those who understood the story were destined for power and those who didn't were sure to lose it.

As a political consultant, I was also well served by the experiences that came from splitting my childhood between two nations. It continues to give me a knack for seeing the world around me as if for the first time, no matter how long I may have spent getting to know a particular place or set of people.

This was partly because I had so frequently been reminded that I was an outsider. As a child, and later when I travelled the world as a consultant, people always ended up asking me one form of the question: "You're not from around here, are you?" It happened so often that part of my mind expected it and prepared for it.

This ability to wipe away the familiar names of things, to always look for the hidden stories, has been a lifelong source of creativity and renewal. Two of my core beliefs about innovation are that it need not be left to chance and that it always begins the moment you see things anew—because that's the moment that we are free to start telling new stories about ourselves. What started as a habit of adjusting myself to the ever-changing circumstances of my life has allowed me to help individuals, companies, nongovernmental organizations (NGOs), and large institutions find their own hidden stories and see themselves anew.

As the careers of Gandhi, Hamilton, and Franklin show, lasting power comes from this process of finding what I call glamour.

So you can think of this book as a guide to uncovering your unique sources of glamour. In this chapter and throughout the book, you'll find useful techniques for finding and telling new stories about yourself or your organization and what to do with those stories once you have them. It's part practical manual and, I hope, part book of spells.

The Power of Stories

Even with data-based approaches, crafting influence, online and off, will always be an art and never a science.

No matter how much data we have about people, and no matter how cunningly we may calibrate the cues that guide them through a digital experience, what governs the final decision to buy an idea or a product will never be completely knowable. This is because people don't completely know themselves.

Consider your own life—from the most trivial objects you've selected for your home to the biggest choices you've made, like whom to marry, where to live, and what career to pursue. Think of the brands you trust and the ones you don't. Can you give a complete accounting of the thoughts and emotions that lead you to say "I do" or sign on the dotted line? Even if you remember the precise moment you made a choice or first believed in something, odds are you can't say exactly what got you there.

As long as we are partly a mystery to ourselves, we will be partly a mystery to every pollster, marketer, data scientist, or advertiser who wants to reach us.

And this is good news for content marketers, because the effectiveness of what we do is based not only on data but on enduring aspects of human nature. Good content, especially compelling stories, sits between science and mystery. Stories command our attention and open our minds to receive new ideas. They aren't effective because they force ideas, but because they awaken our vital needs for wisdom, wonder, and delight.

Wisdom is a distillation of what is useful. And in our accelerated, overmediated present, providing a steady stream of truly useful information is a surefire way to differentiate yourself and elevate your brand.

Wonder stories have been popular as long as humans have been communicating. From ancient myths to superhero movies, people have always craved to know about things that are bigger, faster, more powerful, or just different from their day-to-day experience. Wonder also inherently contains pleasure mixed with the unexpected. We love mysteries because their solutions both surprise and delight us. We love jokes because their punch lines catch us off guard.

To catch the essence of wonder, think of its opposite: boredom. Any topic can be boring if it is presented without surprise. When we know what's going to come next, we're bored. Whenever we have even the slightest reason to guess at what's next, we are on the road to wonder.

This state of consciousness is what your brand should always strive to evoke or be linked to. When people see your logo or hear your brand name, some part of them, however small, should open up to a world of greater possibility.

This Is Your Brain on Good Content

Psychology researchers at Johns Hopkins University discovered that the most favored of over 180 Super Bowl ads were the ones structured like stories. The product or brand being advertised didn't matter. To be loved, an ad only needed this basic structure: a beginning, middle, and end, with some conflict and tension along the way.[1]

---

[1]Jill Rosen, "Super Bowl Ads: Stories Beat Sex and Humor, Johns Hopkins Researcher Finds," January 31, 2014, http://hub.jhu.edu/2014/01/31/super-bowl-ads/.

Stories, even ones assembled from the barest minimum of ingredients, automatically tap into our attention, which is the most precious resource that every product of media and communications—from the biggest Hollywood blockbuster to the lowliest tweet—is in pursuit of. If you can find a way to use your particular medium to tell a story, do it. You are bound to be rewarded with the gift of willing attention.

But attention is not the only state of consciousness that stories are good at evoking. Once you are in the realm of story, your mind is also more trusting. Good stories release a cocktail of neurochemicals in the brain that simultaneously increase focus and empathy. When we are caught up in a good story, our minds are exactly where advertisers want us to be: paying attention and full of good feelings to attach to the focus of that attention.[2] The more empathy we have for somebody, fictional or otherwise, the more we trust that person.

Brain scans reveal that the neural activity of a storyteller is the same as the neural activity of his or her listeners. As neuroscientist Josh Gowin puts it, when we tell stories we are actually taking our thoughts and implanting them in the minds of others.[3]

The hairs pricking up on the back of your neck during a horror film, or the warm feeling that fills your chest at the height of a love story are less intense versions of the same feelings you'd get if you were experiencing those moments firsthand.

This miraculous power isn't science fiction. It's simply the result of words, images, and sounds arranged in the right order.

What's more, there's an increasing amount of evidence that suggests that this synchronization of brain behavior actually translates to lasting empathy. When you share someone's thoughts, the aftereffect

---

[2]Harrison Monarth, "The Irresistible Power of Storytelling as a Strategic Business Tool," *Harvard Business Review*, March 11, 2014, https://hbr.org/2014/03/the-irresistible-power-of-storytelling-as-a-strategic-business-tool.
[3]Josh Gowin, "Why Sharing Stories Brings People Together," *Psychology Today*, June 6, 2011, https://www.psychologytoday.com/blog/you-illuminated/201106/why-sharing-stories-brings-people-together.

is that you are more receptive to the total way they see the world.[4] Stories, then, transfer perspective along with emotion.

It's no mistake that certain vital industries, like finance, energy, and pharma have, as of this writing, some of the steepest reputational battles to win. These industries have been traditionally reticent to share what they do with the world. Decades of self-defensive communications policies have insulated them from scrutiny and kept them safe. But in our fluid and volatile communications environment, safe is not enough. If you are not actively creating a future for your business, you will fall victim to a future created by others. A proactive approach to a reputation is the only truly safe approach.

Tech companies like Facebook and Apple, which are driving the transition to a digital-dominant communications world, have so far done an excellent job, intentionally or not, of telling their own story. It's one in which they are the heroes, channeling the world-changing forces of disruption and innovation to every corner of the economy. The companies of Silicon Valley are now some of the largest in the world, yet the feeling that they are still upstarts battling huge, conservative forces persists. This overarching narrative, which taps into currents of the narrative America tells about itself, has been of high strategic value to the tech industry.

When Apple publicly butted heads with the FBI in 2016 over the company's refusal to provide access to encrypted data on an iPhone, press coverage and public opinion sided quickly and overwhelmingly with Apple. Americans almost instinctively understood that they were siding with the forces of innovation and openness against the forces of tyranny and reaction. More than any factual nuance of the case, and whatever opinion of the case you may have, the overarching innovation story of which Apple has made itself the hero strengthened its negotiating position.

It is not just the ubiquity of its products that makes us feel so comfortable with the tech industry's place in our lives. We also

---

[4]Paul J. Zak, "Why Your Brain Loves Good Storytelling," *Harvard Business Review*, October 28, 2014, https://hbr.org/2014/10/why-your-brain-loves-good-storytelling.

consume medicine, clothing, and energy and use transportation just as frequently as we use our devices. But those industries lack the storytelling capital that Silicon Valley has amassed.

Successful new technologies have always needed stories to usher them into wider social acceptance. You can hear the evidence in our very language.

When we want to change, we talk about turning over a new leaf ("leaf" is an old word for page). When we agree with another person, we're "on the same page."

When our plans go awry, they've been "derailed." When things are on the verge of going well, they're "building up steam," and when they've been going well for a while they're "on track."

Even goofy terms like "blasting off" and "in orbit" are still in use. Each of these phrases has a nostalgic ring now, but when books, railroads, and rockets were first developed, the metaphors I've just listed were still fresh. People took what was exciting about new technology and used it to shape the way they saw moments in their own lives.

The power and the ongoing relevance of Silicon Valley's innovation story can be seen in the freshness of the metaphors it continues to give us. Being "online" is still a good thing both literally and metaphorically. The word "disruption" has flipped its polarity and gone from negative to positive, as has the phrase "going viral." When we figure something out, we've "hacked" it. And now any small, new company, not just tech companies, employs that wonderful bit of self-descriptive poetry, "startup," so close to "upstart" with its inherent promise of insolence and sudden wealth.

These phrases are the atomized pieces of a single dominant Silicon Valley story that has captured the imagination of the world and, for the moment, granted an aura of invincibility to the handful of companies they refer to.

Storytelling, then, represents a remarkable opportunity for any brand that wants to forge or restore its reputation. When a pharmaceutical company, for example, conveys the wonder of curing a disease, or when an energy company chooses a new way to convey the joy of discovering how to power the world, both are sharing the best of what it is like to work there. They are offering pieces of their story to the world to be taken up and disseminated.

A set of self-promotional talking points or the offer of a good deal bounces off the hard shell of skepticism that gets all of us through the day. But pieces of stories have a way of breaking through that shell to become tools that we use to make sense of our own lives.

To fully understand storytelling's power, think of those brands that are quite literally built out of stories—the personal brands of movie stars, musicians, and authors, and the corporate brands of major entertainment companies.

Why is Harry Potter capable of making grown men and women shed their normal state of consciousness and embrace wonder and delight? Because, by consuming J. K. Rowling's stories, many of us have effectively shared the minds and the emotions of her characters. We have lived in their world, and we have contributed our own imaginative resources to its construction. It isn't just Rowling's wonder and delight that we respond to when we read the *Harry Potter* books but our own as well.

Stories make information personal in a way that no other form is capable of. It's a peculiar quirk of our celebrity culture that when we chance to see an actor in person or ask an author to sign our book, we feel as if they should recognize us as an old friend. In a real way, we have actually known them for a long time, but to them we are total strangers. Such is the power of stories to evoke genuine emotion and goodwill once they are released into the world.

This power, even when employed to the smallest degree, is worth a thousand traditional PR plays pushed by TV talking heads or diffused through traditional outlets.

Strategies of Delight

Until now, I've focused on wisdom and wonder.

But the deployment of pure delight is a powerful strategic asset. Along with the quest for power and riches, the simple pursuit of delight has shaped history.

To see what I mean, let's consider a form of delight that is universal and consumed in discrete units, but which is by nature devoid of any messaging: food.

When asked how he planned to restore the international reputation of France, the great diplomat Charles-Maurice de Talleyrand said, "I don't need secretaries as much as I need saucepans!"[5]

Talleyrand was famous for his understanding of how power and influence really work. He was an aristocrat who kept his fortune after the French revolution when most of his peers not only lost their fortunes but also their heads. And he was a politician who worked for every warring faction in France for over 60 years. And in 1814, he pulled off what is still one of the most amazing feats in the history of public relations.

That year, representatives from all over Europe were in Vienna to restore the international order that Napoleon and his French armies had wrecked in 12 years of war. When the post-war government of France needed somebody to represent it in the aftermath, it booked Talleyrand. Think of him as one of the eighteenth and nineteenth centuries' ultimate fixers.

Within months of setting up his new embassy, Talleyrand had dissipated much of the fear and mistrust then directed at France. He gained the trust of the leaders of the German-speaking, English, and Russian alliance that had very recently been France's bitterest enemies. And he came to be seen by smaller nations and ordinary people as a champion of justice.

And he did it all with rich sauces, fine wine, and choice meats. He knew he couldn't best his opponents at the negotiating table outright, so he charmed them at the dining table first. His chef even named dishes after the diplomats they were buttering up, including Nesselrode pudding, named after the Russian ambassador, a rich dessert of cream and alcohol-soaked currants still on the menu in Vienna today.

Like a skilled content strategist, Talleyrand looked deep into his organization, located sources of delight, and made good strategic

———
[5]David King, *Vienna, 1814: How the Conquerors of Napoleon Made Love, War, and Peace at the Congress of Vienna* (New York: Three Rivers Press, 2008), chap. 18.

use of them. Then as now, everybody found high French cooking irresistible, whatever their opinion of the French people.

By the end of the yearlong negotiations, everyone was fighting over invitations to the lavish dinner parties at the French embassy. Talleyrand understood that visceral, positive feelings experienced in the moment can rewrite the pathways of memory. To reset a conversation, he didn't need persuasive ideas or even any ideas at all. He just needed a mechanism to disseminate delight. This is a strategic insight that will never go stale.

Your company cannot and need not literally feed everybody it wants to influence. A steady diet of absorbing stories and useful information is enough. Even in our oversaturated, overcrowded media environment, there will always be room for another good story.

The creation of pure delight, devoid of actual content, is something that content strategists have actually managed to deploy today, with remarkable skill and inventiveness.

In partnership with Rémy Martin's cognac brand Louis XIII, John Malkovich made a film called *The Movie You Will Never See*. Written by Malkovich and directed by Robert Rodriguez, the film was locked in a specially made safe, along with a bottle of Louis XIII. The safe is programmed to open automatically in the year 2117, 100 years—not from the premiere but from the launch party. Three trailers, each imagining a different future, in a range from utopia to dystopia, were released on the Internet.

Perfect for Rémy Martin's purposes, the film provided all the visibility and cachet of a normal cinematic release but without the headache of promoting and distributing the movie, nor, presumably, seeing to its quality.

Articles about the film appeared in *People* and *Entertainment Weekly* and were featured online at *Variety* and the niche sci-fi enthusiast site io9, part of the now-defunct but famous Gawker Media empire. Malkovich gave a series of arch, witty interviews in his signature style, in one of which, mugging for an audience 100 years from now, he declared, "My name *was* John Malkovich."

But most important for the brand, there was a series of parties. The safe, followed by a crew of celebrities, played the role of host of gala receptions starting on a rooftop in Los Angeles and ending at the Cannes Film Festival.

This case is instructive in many ways. It takes an almost goofy idea, a time capsule, and wraps it skillfully in a thick layer of glamour and mystery. But the most important takeaway is this: Content marketing is about convening people around an aspirational idea, one that delights them and inspires them. The ability of *The Movie You Will Never See* to do this without actually providing any content is a fluke—something that only two brands as idiosyncratic as Malkovich and Louis XIII could really pull off, but the lesson is applicable to all content marketers.

Don't underestimate the power of content to convene and to activate far-flung networks simply because of the promise of wonder and delight.

The Runway and the Beltway: Informal Networks of Influence

The case of Talleyrand's saucepan diplomacy illustrates another important point about the advantages of a strategy based on wonder and delight. It activates forces that travel along the informal channels of influence that do so much to govern our lives.

One of the remarkable facts of the so-called Congress of Vienna, the pan-European diplomatic congress that was supposed to vote on a new international order, was that the congress itself never actually convened. Despite a year of being in the same city, the kings, princes, diplomats, and celebrities that gathered there never formally met as one body. The work of the congress, which preserved peace for almost a century, took place behind closed doors and in a succession of glittering balls, dinners, and after parties. Kings and emperors would gather in the morning to hunt, in the afternoon to have lunch, and in the evening at salons, and late at night in trysts and duels. And somehow the work got done.

This is how influence works in our own time, too. We are simply more fond of applying a thick overlay of process and pomp on top of this process. But the reality is that fashion and fun rule over our lives as much as any other set of influences. Influence emanates just as surely from the centers of fashion as it does from the centers of power.

So what does this have to do with content?

Let's start with internal communications—the newsletters, company-wide e-mails, annual reports, and so forth—that we all love to ignore. If crafted to attract attention, these communications can be forces of transformation within your company.

The father of management studies, Peter Drucker, relates how company changes are sold within certain Japanese corporations. The change is announced autocratically from on high, and then all employees are required to handwrite and turn in a document detailing exactly how that change will affect them. And the process is considered done.[6]

This is, of course, the exception that proves the rule, which is that company-wide change is a chaotic, undefined process in most of the rest of the world.

Change is usually driven through a company according to a principle that originated in the discipline of public relations, "third-party credibility." If you want your boss to buy an idea, the best way to start is to make sure he doesn't hear it from you first. If the idea is diffused through the network of people that surround your boss, he'll be prepared for it when it comes.

The great actor Orson Welles had the most amusing version of this principle I've ever heard. When explaining why he took the part of Harry Lime in *The Third Man*, Welles said that it was the perfect example of what he called "the star part." The cast spends all of act one talking about the star part, how mysterious or formidable or grand he is. By the time the character walks on stage, the audience is in such a fever pitch of anticipation that all the actor has to do is mutter a few lines or raise an eyebrow at the right time, and all the intermission chatter is devoted to what an amazing job the actor or actress playing the star part is doing.

---

[6]Peter F. Drucker, *The Daily Drucker* (New York: Harper Business, 2004).

When you want to change your company's reputation or sell an idea, content plays the role of all the characters talking up a star part. Content, because it is inherently sharable, acts like a surrogate member in the various networks of influence within your company. Give them a succession of boring e-mails or, worse, a presentation deck glutted with clichés, and the idea is dead on arrival. But give them stories, and change will spread with all the speed and delight of a particularly dishy rumor.

How Good Content Helps Us Be Our Best Selves

There's a reason big moments in our private and public lives are always accompanied by feasts. When we invite people to our homes to celebrate a marriage, a rite of passage, or a holiday, we also have another motive in mind—creating and sustaining relationships with our family and with friends.

People forge bonds if they're in an open, flexible state of mind, and good food and drink are a reliable way of creating that state of mind.

When we throw a party, we also put on our best clothes, put out the good china, and make sure the house is spotless. It doesn't matter if the house is usually a mess or if we actually prefer a comfy t-shirt and jeans to a suit or a party dress. It is not an act of dishonesty to tidy up and dress up, because parties are an occasion to be our best selves. The same is true of content.

When a company tells its best stories, when it showcases the people in its ranks who are best able to tell those stories, it is putting its best foot forward. By amusing people, informing them, and delighting them, a brand creates the occasion to forge or strengthen a relationship. This convening power of content is unique in the communications landscape.

As of this writing, the most valuable brand in the world is Disney. As a company, Disney doesn't clothe us, put a roof over our heads, keep us safe, or feed us from day to day. It does one thing supremely well. Disney delights and surprises us. Whenever children and adults who have a history with the brand see Mickey Mouse's silhouette, their minds and hearts open up. They enter an altered state of consciousness, in which they are willing to spend money on something nonessential—because they know that by doing so they're accepting an invitation, for however brief a duration, to the never-ending banquet of Disney's content.

Disney's theme parks are literal feasting grounds. People convene their families there to celebrate milestones. They eat good food, share experiences, and consume great stories together. The brand tagline may be about storybook magic, but Disney's real magic is the relationships it helps sustain.

Content Creates Guiding Narratives

Some of our most important work is to help each other construct guiding narratives, big-picture stories that make sense of the world and define our place in it.

Imagine yourself sitting down to watch a friend's favorite TV show. Unless your friend explains the show's guiding narrative—the big-picture story—the names and events of a particular episode won't make much sense.

We do something similar every day, but in our own lives and with much higher stakes questions like: How do I do my job? What will the world be like in the near future? How should I spend my time and money?

The more long-term context we have about everything, the more confidence we have in answering those questions.

Guiding narratives used to be dictated by the received wisdom of our culture, which was a blend of family history, national history, folklore, and religion. By the time we grew up, we knew our place in the world. And by the time we grew old, it hadn't changed that much. All the good and bad events in our lives were reconciled in one guiding narrative. Even if life was difficult or confusing, we had a larger context of meaning to fit it into.

With the fragmentation of experience, including our media, guiding narratives aren't a given anymore. We have to piece them together ourselves from the bits of information that float to us on the streams of information we all swim in.

For anybody crafting a reputation, either for themselves or for a company, this is important to remember. Unless you make the raw ingredients of your big-picture story available, either to your friends and family, your potential customers, or the public in general, they'll use whatever they have to construct their own guiding narrative about you. Even without realizing it, people are always making up stories in their heads and casting elements of the world around them as characters. It's something that's going to happen with or without your input.

For companies, this means you've got to get the right knowledge about your brand out there in the form of stories that people absorb and share. In the age of atomized content, where every story might be split up into pieces as small as a phrase or a single image, or assembled into long-form articles or video pieces, having a master brand narrative in mind—one that everybody in your company can use—is crucial.

One beneficial effect of this guiding narrative is that it reduces the challenge of creating small pieces of content or responding in the moment to what seem like isolated communications challenges. With a clear guiding narrative, choosing an image or a few words for an Instagram post, for example—something that can eat up a surprising amount of time and mental energy—gets a lot easier. If you are, for example, a large agricultural company that wants to emphasize the wonder and discovery that goes into growing and harvesting food, then just having those keywords in mind is enough of an idea to keep a steady stream of content flowing. Guiding narratives are where strategy begins.

The context provided by a guiding narrative extends to your audience, too, not just your company's story.

A content marketing strategy is optimized for the creation of master brand narratives in our atomized media environment, because it allows people to approach content in their own way. When they tap into a social media feed, the raw elements of your story will be there. When they do web searches, the same thing will be true. And the task of remixing it and assembling it is the creative act of each individual user—it's not imposed from on high.

It's important to remember, too, that the job of assembling your guiding narrative is something undertaken not only by everybody who works to forge your brand image but also by every piece of content. No individual has the task of hitting all your messaging in a single communication.

Where do guiding narratives live?

They begin in collaboration. Start by convening people from throughout your company who have key elements of its story. While it's important to have buy-in from people at the top of the hierarchy, it's equally important not to stop there.

Don't be afraid to cast (literally cast, as a fisherman does with his line and hook) deep and wide into your organization. Look for what business writer Michael D. Watkins calls "natural company historians." This can be anybody from a long-time, trusted administrative assistant to your chief marketing officer.

It's the informal networks of influence that you want to tap into, not just the official org chart. Be sure to look for people whose job it is to tell your company's story on a regular basis, like the head of corporate social responsibility or experienced salespeople. If you're savvy enough to have an in-house content marketing team, they're an obvious invite.

Once you've got your cast of characters, get them together for a planned exploration of your company's story. Planned is not the same as formal. In our experience we find that informal works better. Depending on the client, we've found that different things can loosen minds and tongues and get the stories flowing. We've planned workshops built around arts and crafts, drawing, painting, dancing, festive food, and even, in some cases, alcohol.

The goal is the creation of a document that can eventually be shared with everybody whose job is to be public-facing. We've also found that it's best to think of the guiding narrative as a living document, something to be revised yearly or quarterly. We've seen it function as something of an informal company newsletter, but one that employees actually want to read. It's a way for each department to put its best foot forward in the form of new stories and proof points. The guiding narrative's job is to keep information flowing throughout your organization, to generate ideas for content marketing, and to form the raw materials for the image you want to broadcast to the world.

What's Old Is New Again

In its current digital incarnation, content marketing is truly something new under the sun. The continuous diffusion of messaging throughout different platforms combined with real-time feedback about what works has never before been possible.

But in its essence, content marketing is what was practiced in the so-called golden age of advertising, which coincided with the rise of legends like Bill Bernbach and David Ogilvy. Both were committed to creating beautiful, interesting, and informative pieces of communication. And both were committed to elevating the conversation rather than reducing the craft to the quick and easy attractions of either sex or the manipulations of direct marketing.

Turn to the introduction of Ogilvy's most famous book, still one of the best books ever written about strategic communications, *Ogilvy on Advertising*, and you won't find a quote from the *Harvard Business Review* or statistics from market research. You'll find a quote from the ancient Athenian orator and statesman Demosthenes. Elsewhere in the book you'll see an ad for a shipping company that quotes the philosopher Epictetus, and another that explains the religious customs of Singapore. The book is filled with examples that provide delight and wisdom in at least equal parts to persuasion. And on every page you'll see ads that look and read like articles—content marketing long before its time.

What SJR, the innovation consultancy I cofounded, does is to take these core principles and apply them to what's possible in the digital age. We are no longer constrained by space as we were in the era of print advertising. We move faster. And we are no longer reliant on paying the advertising rates charged by publications for the distribution of content. But the core strategy of relentlessly crafting communications that never go out into the world without being of benefit to the reader remains as effective as it was half a century ago.

How to Find Good Stories

TAKE ME TO YOUR LEADER

The practice of content marketing is essentially alien to the way most corporations operate. One member of my firm even describes the process of launching a content strategy as akin to mounting a benevolent alien invasion.

After convincing the relevant leader in marketing, corporate communications, or some other department that content is the best way forward, there is that inevitable first interaction with a company.

You show up with your crew of photographers, writers, journalists, filmmakers, and artists, and you start to poke your head into what's going on in search of stories that will inform and delight the public and the company's customers.

This process involves asking a lot of questions about how different parts of the company interact (or don't). It also means asking a lot of seemingly stupid questions about a company's products, which may have been answered internally so long ago that they seem obvious.

Coming in under an agency banner can excuse some of this behavior, even have it come across as the charming eccentricity of "creative types." If you are an in-house marketer or communicator attempting to implement a content strategy, you won't have this advantage.

My advice for you and for your team is to lean in to the strangeness and awkwardness of this initial phase. It can only help you. It is precisely your freshness of mind that makes you valuable.

When you come in asking funny, authentic questions, people don't know what to make of you. If they don't have a category to put your questions in, they won't have a category for you, either, and that can get you through doors that wouldn't otherwise open for you. Young children wield this power without realizing it. Driven by pure curiosity, they are unafraid to ask questions to any person, and their curiosity is indulged. And just as with young children, indulging the question can change the questioned as much as the questioner.

SJR is an innovation consultancy, and one of our key areas of specialty is that we have no specific area of specialty. We make a point of hiring from every field. We have lawyers, management consultants, filmmakers, journalists, writers, advertising creatives, experts in policy, graphic and fine artists, musicians, and people from the world of philanthropy and nonprofit organizations. And one of the things I love to do is toss one or two people onto a team with little to no experience of the client's industry. It always yields new insights and crisp ways of reimagining things.

In the Middle Ages, when there was bad news to give to the king, they often called in the court jester. Because he expected jokes and not substantive news, the king was more likely to actually listen to that news, and less likely to cut off anybody's head because of it.

Sometimes I think of SJR as performing the function of court jesters. Because we are storytellers, we have a kind of license to tell the truth to the people in charge.

Sometimes I think of us as being like children who don't yet have names for the things they see and are therefore better able to understand them. And sometimes we are like aliens on a new planet, discovering it for the first time.

PLAY UP

By bringing your company up to speed, content marketing done right provides a valuable service. We force you to reexamine and hone your purpose, and we help you become agile because you don't have time to be otherwise.

Content marketing forces its practitioners to become some combination of detectives, storytellers, and tricksters. To turn your company into a story with speed, we invite you to play a sort of game. And like all games, the prize is real self-knowledge without the cost of real-world failure.

If you don't have the ability to hire an outside agency to kick-start your content marketing efforts, one thing you can do is cultivate an outsider's attitude by asking this simple question: Where in our company are people having the most fun?

This may not be any officially approved endeavor. It is likely to be a passion project of a few dedicated employees or an idea that seems way ahead of its time.

But there are two reasons fun is likely to be the source of a great story. The first is that fun is where people naturally make new connections within themselves and forge lasting relationships with others. According to Stuart Brown's book *Play*, games are where we learn as children most authentically who we are and where we, quite literally, learn how to play with others and where we fit in. In a company context, this means that playful activities, like clubs, sports teams, or side projects are where you're going to find the real stories and real relationships that mark out how your company really does business.

Another reason that fun is a good place to look for stories is that it tends to be a good predictor of the future of a business. The steam engine, the submarine, the internal combustion engine, robots, and computers all started out as side projects or toys that serious inventors made for fun and amusement, either their own or others.[7]

GETTING THE STORY APPROVED

Inevitably, it's the best stories that are most in danger of getting killed off in the approval process.

That is entirely understandable. Stories are memorable, and the job of in-house public affairs, public relations, or corporate communications departments is to protect the brand. And one sure way to do it is to deflect attention and minimize interest. But a safe, conservative approach will only get you so far.

---

[7]Steven Johnson, *Wonderland: How Play Made the Modern World* (New York: Riverhead Books, 2016), 1–15.

You can't restore a reputation or transform one unless you take action. And in the world of communications, stories are the most effective action you can take.

Let's look at two common pitfalls to avoid.

1. Putting Too High a Burden on Every Piece of Content. Like the famous anecdote about the sculptor (often suggested to be Michelangelo) who, when asked how he carved such a perfect statue of an elephant replied, "I simply take out all the pieces of stone that are not an elephant," the content marketer's job is to know what to leave out.

An entrenched communications team is likely to want every outgoing message from the company to hit every major messaging point and respond to every current of discussion in the public sphere. This is always a mistake. To be captivating, a story has to create something like a self-contained universe. And this means leaving a lot of seemingly essential things out.

As Voltaire said, "To be a bore, one merely has to say everything."

2. Analysis Paralysis. Velocity, the quality of moving with both speed and intention, is essential to any good content strategy. The Internet is built for speed and for a site to stay relevant, it needs a steady supply of stories.

Marketing and communications departments that are used to being reactive may have fully bought into a content-based strategy and yet still unconsciously kill off its chances of success by passing stories along to every stakeholder before they are finally approved. If newspapers and daily news sites behaved this way, the public would forever be uninformed and unamused.

Involving too many stakeholders in the approval process can also risk making your ideas muddled. As the saying goes, "a camel is a horse designed by committee." If you want good stories told at speed, give them to a few trusted people who care about the brand and have access to a few high-level stakeholders capable of keeping things moving. Consensus can be necessary for certain decisions, but when it comes to stories, velocity and a coherent vision are far more important.

Insights

- Data-based approaches can help us influence hearts and minds, but intangibles, like wisdom, wonder, and delight will always move people in ways that can never be quantified.
- Stories are reliable sources of wonder, wisdom, and delight and have been for all of human history.
- For a brand to convene people and create lasting influence, it needs to tell stories.

Ask Yourself

- In what way is my brand telling its own story? In what ways has it allowed others to tell that story?
- What sources of delight exist within my company that the world should know about? That other employees should know about?
- Is my company's strategy based on laying low and avoiding criticism, or is it based on forging a narrative that people can relate to and take up?

2

The Age of the Educated Consumer

Why Politics Won't Teach You about Marketing

The path from politics to marketing and strategic communications is a common one. It is the path my own career and the careers of some of my most respected colleagues have taken. In some ways, the crucible of politics is excellent preparation for marketing. Working on campaigns teaches you that a communications strategy has the power to shape reality, first in the minds of voters and then in the real-world effects of policy. It teaches you that reputation and brand can be both durable and fickle. A single well-phrased comment can make or break a political reputation, but it can also pass by entirely unnoticed in the stream of political life. Working in politics also teaches you that branding and reputation is an endurance activity. You learn how to work well when you are tired, to work without complete information, and to improvise, improvise, improvise.

An early major donor to Bill Clinton's first presidential campaign once related to me how Clinton, then a relative naïf in the realm of foreign policy, sat and listened to him talk off the cuff about the state of nuclear policy with China. Later that evening, when Clinton was asked in a round of public questions to expound on exactly that issue, he was able to take the donor's disorganized thoughts and turn them into a coherent speech that did not sound extemporaneous and that left the room dazzled. This same improvisational ability is invaluable in the world of marketing.

But there are only so many lessons and skills that transfer from politics. Just because a tactic wins in the all-or-nothing warfare of politics does not mean that it will win over hearts and minds in the long game of marketing and branding.

If that were true, you would see content marketing in politics. And it is a remarkable yet totally understandable fact that you don't see it at all. The reason for this is that in a political campaign, the education of voters is a liability.

In warfare, victory goes to those who can choose the site of battle. The equivalent of that in communications is defining the terms of the debate. When you educate a voter—about the issues, about the larger context of a candidate's life—you inevitably reduce your strategic advantage by increasing the number of battlefields where you have to defend your candidate's reputation. The more context you have, the more sophisticated your strategy has to be.

It is a lamentable fact that the less informed voters are, the easier they are swayed. In the 2016 U.S. presidential election, despite decades in the public eye, Hillary Clinton's deep breadth of public service accomplishments were swept away by Donald Trump's single, bullying phrase, "crooked Hillary." This tactical dumbing down of voters is skilled warfare, but it is the opposite of content marketing.

In politics, there is always an inflection point on the horizon—the next election day. That is all that matters.

But in marketing and branding, there is never a natural inflection point on the horizon. The reputational game is long and diffuse. Combative, focused ploys like "crooked Hillary" are designed for short-term wins. They wear thin too fast to be of lasting value. Even Trump himself expressed this when, after winning the election, he interrupted audiences chanting his anti-Hillary slogans. That played well in the campaign, Trump said, but we're not going to carry it forward into the work of actually governing.

The act of governing—the long series of decisions that have to be made—is much closer to what managing a corporate reputation is most like. It is less a war than a game, and one with shifting rules at that. It is not a zero-sum game but an open-ended one. The goal is not just to win any battles that come along but to create an entire world in which battles are more easily won. It is about creating a lasting picture of reality in the minds of consumers in which your brand occupies a positive place.

And if people do not know your brand and what it does for the world, this is an impossible task. In the world of long-term brand building, the only winning strategy is one where you smarten up, never dumb down.

The Educated Consumer

The advent of every communications technology was accompanied by fears that it would make us dumber or somehow change what it means to be human, usually for the worse.

Socrates, speaking in the increasingly literate environment of ancient Athens, complained that by writing things down, people would lose their memories and would be less capable of making new knowledge a working part of who they were.

The outbreak of mass print literacy in Europe starting in the late 1700s was accompanied by predictions that it would disintegrate the moral fiber of civilization and lead to mass chaos. The same has been true at the start of telegraphy, telephones, radio, television, the Internet, and now mobile technology.

And it's true that the way we communicate does change how we think. We do rely less on our memories and more on our ability to organize or call up information than did somebody in ancient Greece. And we are learning more and learning it faster, and we are replacing that body of knowledge continuously rather than only during the parts of our lives set apart for education.

But far from making us dumber, there is evidence that we are actually getting smarter. In an effect observed for over a century and in more than 30 countries, scores on IQ tests have been increasing at a rate of about three points per decade[1] for the past century.

This is not the result of IQ tests getting easier. Evidence suggests that they have actually been getting harder. This trend is a result of many factors, including better nutrition, the eradication of many brain- and body-crippling diseases, and, I suspect, the wider availability of good information to those who want to find it, as well as the steady, inexorable march of more widely available education.[2]

Key to note is that this is not an effect limited to the developing world. It is also measurable in Europe and the United States just as much as in Latin America, Asia, and Africa. People really are getting smarter, especially in the area of abstract reasoning.[3]

In the United States at least, this is accompanied by an increase in reading, especially among millennials. Despite the perception that our attention is becoming hopelessly fragmented and that people have lost a taste for long-form, informative content, the reverse is true. People are reading more now than they ever have before. And those under the age of 30 are reading slightly more than those over

---

[1]Tom Chivers, "The Flynn Effect: Are We Really Getting Smarter?" *The Telegraph*, October 31, 2014, www.telegraph.co.uk/news/science/science-news/11200900/The-Flynn-effect-are-we-really-getting-smarter.html.
[2]Ibid.
[3]Ibid.

the age of 30, both online and off.[4] E-book consumption has evened out in the high, single-digit percentage of the population, print book consumption has increased, and reading on cell phones, tablets, and computers has jumped considerably.[5]

Most important of all for the content marketer is this fact: the number one reason that people read content of any kind in any format is to research a specific topic that interests them.

Of American adults, 84 percent read for the purpose of research, compared to 82 percent to keep up with the news, 80 percent for pleasure, and 57 percent who read for school.[6] Even with the massive textbook market and the perceived drop-off in reading that happens when we graduate from school, the fact remains that when people want to learn, they turn to content.

And when it comes to content that is not on Twitter or Facebook, people tend to read long. The ideal length for a blog post is 1,600 words, which is, on average, about a six-minute read.[7] And the most-shared stories on major news sites tend to be either very short, about 200 words, or much heftier, closer to 2,000 words.[8] People want a small bite of information or a deep dive.

And, as with any product or brand, people tend to turn to certain information sources when they go through a particular life event. According to Pew, events like the birth of a child or starting a new job can spark lasting relationships with libraries.[9]

---

[4]Adrienne LaFrance, "Millennials Are Out-Reading Older Generations," *The Atlantic*, September 10, 2014, www.theatlantic.com/technology/archive/2014/09/millennials-are-out-reading-older-generations/379934/

[5]Pew Research Center Internet, Science & Tech, "Book Reading 2016," September 1, 2016, http://www.pewinternet.org/2016/09/01/book-reading-2016/.

[6]Ibid.

[7]Kevan Lee, "Infographic: The Optimal Length for Every Social Media Update," October 21, 2014, https://blog.bufferapp.com/optimal-length-social-media.

[8]Liam Corcoran, "I Thought Long Form Was Dead—Then I Saw These Awesome Stats," December 12, 2013, https://www.newswhip.com/2013/12/article-length/#CeH4JWhQOUhJrJ2q.99.

[9]Kathryn Zickugr, Kristen Purcell, and Lee Raine. *From Distant Admirers to Library Lovers—and Beyond A Typology of Public Library Engagement in America.* Pew Research Center, March 13, 2014, www.pewinternet.org/2014/03/13/library-engagement-typology/.

When you satisfy the considerable desire for content that truly informs, it creates the possibility for enduring reader relationships that can, in turn, lead to a flourishing relationship with your company.

The case of Everplans, a confidential data storage website organized around major life events, is a great example. The site's co-founders, Abby Schneiderman and Adam Seifer, came up with the idea for their business when they discovered that there was no centralized online resource for end-of-life planning, a fact made especially painful after Schneiderman's brother passed away suddenly in 2010. By 2012, the pair had launched Everplans and by 2015, over two million people had visited it to consume its useful, niche content. That translated into 15,000 subscribers to the site's digital vault service,[10] and the company has now entered the business-to-business market, launching cobranding deals with insurance companies and HR departments.

The takeaway is that the business model was born from a desire to fill a void in the world's knowledge.

It is Everplans' 2,500-plus freely available articles that are the reason the service is thriving, not its data storage technology. People came for the content and stayed for the business.

For legacy brands looking to maintain their reputations in our start-up and innovation-obsessed market, content isn't just an opportunity but a necessity. If you are, say, an established transportation company, a maker of automobiles or locomotives, it isn't enough to digitize your business. If your trains are capable of optimizing routes or fuel usage or your cars are capable of the same or more, you have an opportunity to be seen as an innovator by sharing your discoveries with the world. Consumers and industry peers will look to you for knowledge, and when the time comes to look to you for business, their minds will naturally turn the same way.

For start-ups, the benefits of educating consumers are even more pronounced, because the burden is so much higher. You don't just have to build brand awareness, or even product awareness, you also have to tell the world what your product is and what it can do.

---

[10]"45/46 Abby Schneiderman and Adam Seifer, Cofounders and Co-CEOs, Everplans," *Fast Company*, May 24, 2016.

You cannot rely on the rest of the media ecosystem to socialize a new technology for you.

And with both legacies and start-ups, the pressure to make your content not only useful but smart is increasing as consumers themselves get smarter.

We are truly living and doing business in the age of the educated consumer.

Insights

- In the game of brand reputation, unlike politics, there are no planned victories or defeats in the form of periodic elections. You have to decide what your own standards of success and failure will be, and measure accordingly.
- In a totally on-demand communications environment, where people don't have to watch what's scheduled, the advantage goes to those who try to elevate or smarten up the conversation, not dumb it down.
- There is no ideal medium for your content. Each one has its drawbacks and unique advantages.

Ask Yourself

- What assumptions am I making about the media habits of the people who care about my brand? Where can I go to validate or challenge those assumptions?
- What are three things I wish people knew about my organization or company?
- Take 15 minutes and look at the content on your website. Is it useful to the reader? Is it informative?

3

It's about Human Nature

We are born helpless. As soon as we are fully conscious we discover lone-
liness. We need others physically, emotionally, intellectually; we need
them if we are to know anything, even ourselves.

—C. S. Lewis

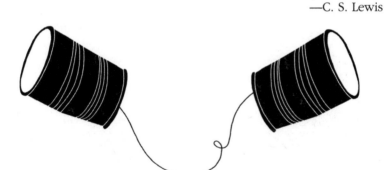

A s social beings, we have an evolutionary need to communicate and connect with other people. Each of us strives to belong to a group and bond with people, the same way we have a basic need for food and shelter.

Matthew D. Lieberman, a neuroscientist and educator who leads the Social Cognitive Neuroscience Lab at UCLA Department of Psychology, sees the brain as the center of our social selves. In his book *Social: Why Our Brains Are Wired to Connect*, he hypothesizes that our brains evolved to experience threats to our social connections in the same way they evolved to experience physical pain. Emotional pain and physical pain are inextricably linked, which explains why parents have a need to keep their kids close, and why we hold on to our intimate relationships over time. When something goes wrong with a loved one, it activates neural circuitry that can cause us to feel physical pain in the chest—heartbreak. This reaction was born out of an evolutionary need to stay socially connected over the course of our lives, Lieberman contends.

Other research emphasizes the health benefits of being connected; one study[1] showed that a lack of social connection is a greater detriment to health than obesity, smoking, and high blood pressure. Social bonds actually strengthen our immune systems, as research from UCLA School of Medicine's Steve Cole shows that the same genes impacted by social connection also code for immune function and inflammation,[2] which is why having connections help us recover from disease faster, and may even lengthen our lives.[3] People with healthy relationships have higher self-esteem, are more empathic to others, more trusting and cooperative and, as a consequence, others are more open to trusting and cooperating with them, according to studies.[4]

Communication allows us to feel connected and helps us better understand ourselves, which is why storytelling has been an inherent, universal part of the human experience.

You can trace it back thousands of years to the days of the shaman, who told stories and sang songs around a tribal fire, conveying the history of the tribe; important news about people within

[1]J. S. House, K. R. Landis, and D. Umbersom, "Social Relationships and Health," *Science.* July 29, 1988, http://science.sciencemag.org/content/241/4865/540.
[2]Viviane Callier, "Climbing the Social Ladder Can Strengthen Your Immune System, Monkey Study Suggests," *Science.* November 24, 2016, www.sciencemag.org/news/2016/11/climbing-social-ladder-can-strengthen-your-immune-system-monkey-study-suggests.
[3]Patrick L. Hill and Nicholas A Turiano. "Purpose in Life as a Predictor of Mortality Across Adulthood," *Sage*, May 8, 2014. http://journals.sagepub.com/doi/abs/10.1177/0956797614531799.
[4]Richard M. Lee, Matthew Draper, and Sujin Lee, "Social Connectedness, Dysfunctional Interpersonal Behaviors, and Psychological Distress: Testing a Mediator Model," *APA PsycNET*, July 2001, http://psycnet.apa.org/index.cfm?fa=buy.optionToBuy&id=2001-07409-008.

it; and establishing the beliefs, values, and rules of the group. The shaman's ability to communicate to the tribe (and with the metaphysical world, connecting with spirits and relaying their messages to the larger group) led people to believe that his stories, chants, and prayers had healing powers that could cure a range of ailments.

Years later, religious leaders became our predominant storytellers and healers, delivering stories from religious texts, consoling members of the community one-on-one, and using prayer to heal.

And then it became musicians, poets, writers, and on-stage performers who became the storytellers. Over the course of history, people have sat up and taken notice of the storytellers who are able to tap into the human experience, whether it was Homer, with his epic poems in the eighth century BC, Dante Alighieri's masterpiece *Divine Comedy* in the early fourteenth century, or Shakespeare delivering a play on stage in the late sixteenth century.

These authors have endured today—as part of literature curricula—because of how the authors explored fundamental aspects of our existence. In Shakespeare's case, his plays and sonnets evoke a full range of our emotions and awaken our senses, through his presentation of timeless, relatable themes such as ambition, betrayal, revenge, jealousy, dreams, appearance versus reality, and difficulty in love. Human stories like that don't lose their magnetism, even centuries later.

In fact, directors, actors, and writers find so much value in these stories that they've adapted them in countless ways for audiences today (think of all the different versions of *Romeo and Juliet*, *Macbeth*, *The Taming of the Shrew*, and *Othello* that exist).

Today, you can find talented storytellers in every corner of our popular culture, and they've tapped into the same elemental aspects of human existence as the great authors of our time have. Prolific songwriter and producer Max Martin, for example, has written many of the mega pop hits that get played so much on the radio (ones we're embarrassed to admit we know all the words to), including "...Baby One More Time" by Britney Spears, "As Long as You Love Me" by the Backstreet Boys, "Bad Blood" by Taylor Swift and "I Kissed a Girl" by Katy Perry to name just a few. Love or hate those songs, Martin's gift in writing relatable lyrics that we can't seem forget is undeniable.

Martin is a masterful translator of human experience, taking emotion and common sentiments and transforming them into song.

Pollster Nate Silver is another a talented translator, turning raw data into totally original, breaking news stories about politics, sports, science and health, and culture with his website FiveThirtyEight. Steven Spielberg is a translator in film, enthralling his audience in 1975 with *Jaws* as much as he did with *E.T. the Extra-Terrestrial* in 1982, and *Saving Private Ryan* in 1998 through his incredible ability to build intricate worlds for his characters. And famed photographer Annie Leibovitz can be seen as a translator, developing a strong rapport with each of her subjects to create deeply personal, intimate windows into the lives of people like John Lennon.

What can we learn from all of these examples? Every form of storytelling, whether it's a portrait, film, political speech, a musical performance, a religious sermon, a novel, a documentary or anything else, *must be human in order to be great.* The same holds true for marketing and advertising; *you can't create desire without understanding what humans desire, and you can't shape a reputation without understanding how people think.*

When approaching a new campaign or project, you need to think about the humans consuming your work *before* you think about the brand—this holds true whether you're a copywriter, a creative director, a brand journalist, videographer, graphic designer, or strategist.

Parts of the Internet have become a wasteland. Or, as I'm increasingly fond of saying, "The problem with the Internet is that it's boring."

What I'm referring to: clickbait headlines, articles so stuffed with keywords that they say nothing, horrible stock photos, and the dumbed-down articles that have been churned out *ad nauseum.* Think of *The 7 Habits of Highly Effective People*-style posts you see on so many online platforms.

The people responsible for such work are trying to game online search, or making safe bets by following the lead of other authors and rehashing the same thoughts. Some brands take the same unimaginative, uninspiring approach to content, solely focused on page views and unique visitors, when engagement and repeat visitors are arguably more important, because anyone can get eyeballs on a site (especially with a massive paid distribution budget), but few can sustain a community of engaged readers or create the kind of content that gets republished by other outlets.

The truth is, if you're doing the same content everyone else has done and praying your highly paid SEO specialist will save you, you've already lost. No one will remember your work or want to come back to your website if they've landed there.

It's human stories that are accessible but elevated that people remember. So aim to smarten your audience up, and tell stories in creative ways with as much attention to the visual vocabulary as the text. You'll earn your audience's trust, which is as valuable as currency.

Unsurprisingly, we can learn a lot from skilled public speakers about how to gain public trust and shape opinion. The best orators in history captured the power of human storytelling using emotional words and delivery that brought people solace during difficult times and hope for a better future. For marketers, it's worth exploring what they did to capture the hearts and minds of their audiences.

Learning from the Best Human Storytellers

1. *Tailor your story for the situation and medium.* You'll never hear someone like Barack Obama tell the same story the same way more than once. The way he shared his vision for the country and his personal story when he was running for president in 2008 was different when he was in front of a crowd of blue-collar automotive industry workers in Michigan than when he stood before big-time donors at a political fundraising dinner. The best storytellers know that you can't talk to everyone the same way. Online, with a multitude of storytelling media at your disposal, this becomes even more important with different audiences on each platform and tools at your fingertips. You wouldn't post the same thing on Twitter as you would on Tumblr, and you wouldn't run the same native advertisement on the *New York Times* website as you would in New York Magazine. Figure out who your audience is and speak their language.

2. *Know when to speak.* "Well-timed silence hath more eloquence than speech," said the English writer and poet Martin Farquhar Tupper. Timing is everything. Franklin D. Roosevelt began his fireside chats in 1933, amid a recession and banking crisis—one in four Americans was unemployed, and in some cities, unemployment was well over 50 percent.[5] Some 9,000 banks had closed, with $2.5 billion in lost deposits. Americans were panicked about the future. Many didn't understand what was happening or the steps FDR and legislators were taking to pull the country out of its deep slump. It was time for the leader to restore the public's confidence. In these weekly radio addresses, FDR discussed his New Deal initiatives in an informal, conversational way. He used easy-to-grasp examples and analogies to explain what was going on and his plan to rebuild. But it wasn't dumbed down; given the length of words and sentences Roosevelt used, he was speaking at a near-college level compared with the eighth-grade level of speech used by modern-day presidents, according to Elvin Lim, an assistant professor of government at Wesleyan University.[6] Roosevelt's chats succeeded because, more than anything, he had in mind the human beings on the other end of the radio. He began his addresses with "My friends," not "American citizens." At the end of his first chat, he said this, which really drove his message home: "After all, there is an element in the readjustment of our financial system more important than currency, more important than gold, and that is the confidence of the people themselves. Confidence and courage are the essentials of success in carrying out our plan. You people must have faith; you must not be stampeded by rumors or guesses. Let us unite in banishing fear. We have provided the machinery to restore our financial system; and it is up to you to support and make it work. It is your problem, my friends, your problem no less than it is mine. Together we cannot fail." His fireside chats were exactly what Americans needed at the time—thousands

---

[5]History.com staff, "The Fireside Chats," *A+E Network*, http://www.history.com/topics/fireside-chats.
[6]Eileen Ambrose, "FDR's Fireside Chats Went a Long Way toward Calming Fears During Dire Times," *The Baltimore Sun*, October 19, 2008, http://articles.baltimoresun.com/2008-10-19/business/0810190058_1_vanden-heuvel-fireside-chats-roosevelt-served.

wrote to him to thank him for breaking down complexities at an uncertain time.[7]

3. *Prepare obsessively.* Like an Oscar-winning director thinks through every detail of a film before releasing it to the public, or an artist painstakingly reviews each and every centimeter of a piece of work, a great storyteller spends hours, days, and months preparing before unveiling a story to the public. Every single word matters. How long should a presentation take to prepare for? Longer than you think. According to Nancy Duarte, the communications expert behind Al Gore's *An Inconvenient Truth*, for an hour-long presentation, presenters should spend roughly 30 hours researching, organizing, sketching, storyboarding, scripting, and revising. Then, an additional 30 hours building visual materials, such as slides, and then another 30 hours rehearsing the delivery. Yup, that's 90 hours of preparation for a mere 60 minutes. Sounds crazy, right? But think of how successful Gore's film was in putting climate change not just at the forefront of the American conversation but the global one, too.

Steve Jobs also took a meticulous, painstaking approach to preparing for his presentations. Jobs storyboarded the plot of his speeches, planned each word in detail, created presentation slides himself, reviewed product demos repeatedly, rehearsed his every move on stage and even planned for on-stage technical failures. Appearing unfazed when his clicker failed, Jobs was in the habit of having a personal story memorized as he was waiting for his team to fix the issue so he could get on with his presentation.

With all of this planning, Jobs kept his audiences engaged the entire time, surprising them, making them laugh, and inspiring them with the power of technology. Audience members walked away believing in the power of Apple products to revolutionize the world, thanks to Jobs' theatrics and skillful delivery. During his keynotes, he avoided getting into technical specs, preferring to speak in human terms that anyone in his audience could understand; he described the iPod as "one thousand songs in your pocket" rather than "a tiny 6.5-ounce portable music player with 5G of storage."

---

[7] Ibid.

Accept that your best work will take a lot of time to create and a lot of hours reviewing, revising, and collaborating with other talented people. It can't be rushed. In marketing, and strategic communications, we don't always have time on our side, but whenever possible, push back on deadlines and shift projects to other people to allow your team members to really focus on one project at a time. It will show in the quality of your work.

4. *But remain flexible.* Did you know that Martin Luther King Jr.'s famous "I Have a Dream" speech was not scripted? He had prepared a speech, but 10 minutes in, decided to put it aside and skipped whole paragraphs. Mahalia Jackson, who had performed earlier and was one of King's favorite gospel singers, cried, "Tell 'em about the dream, Martin!" according to Drew Hansen, author of *The Dream*. He then said, "I say to you today my friends, even though we face the difficulties of today and tomorrow, I still have a dream. It is a dream deeply rooted in the American dream. It is a dream that one day this nation will rise up and live out the true meaning of its creed: 'We hold these truths to be self-evident, that all men are created equal.'" As applause grew and began to drown him out, he raised his voice and said, "I have a dream that someday on the red hills of Georgia, the sons of former slaves and the sons of former slave owners will be able to sit down together at the table of brotherhood." He returned to the script just for the closing line: "Free at last, free at last, thank God Almighty—we are free at last!" It was not the first time King said, "I have a dream"—he had used it a few times earlier that year—but it was by far his most well-received.

"I started out reading the speech, and I read it down to a point, and just all of a sudden I decided—the audience response was wonderful that day, you know—and all of a sudden this thing came to me that I'd used many times before, that thing about 'I have a dream.' I just felt I wanted to use it. I don't know why. I hadn't thought about it before that speech," King told Donald Smith, a graduate student, later that year.[8]

---

[8]Rick Hampson, "What You Didn't Know about King's 'Dream' Speech," *USA Today*. August 12, 2013, www.usatoday.com/story/news/nation/2013/08/12/march-on-washington-king-speech/2641841/.

As an orator, King was operating in a great tradition of African-American preaching, in which improvisation and sudden inspiration played a central role. In this tradition, long hours absorbing the powerful cadences of the King James Bible and dissecting the finer points of theology, politics, and justice are meant to be brought together in unexpected, eloquent patterns of speech improvised in a public setting. By deviating from his planned speech, King was taking a chance, but he was also playing to his strengths. In a sense, he'd been preparing for that moment his entire life.

When you've prepared and you're passionate about your message and feel you have something truly important to say, just say it; odds are the world will listen.

You don't always have to stick to a script, and it doesn't always have to be perfect; some of the best messages materialize in the moment. King's core message was simple, emotional, and raw—all elements of a compelling human story.

5. *Know your audience; have self-awareness.* In 1588, English troops stationed at Tilbury Fort readied for an expected invasion by the Spanish Armada. As someone who was always extremely deliberate in her words and her public approach, Queen Elizabeth I rallied the troops with one of the most powerful speeches of her career. She gave it while wearing a plumed helmet and a steel cuirass over a white velvet gown. Holding a gold and silver baton as she rode atop a white steed, historians say her look was deliberately reminiscent of several powerful female literary and mythological figures, including Pallas Athena, the Greek goddess of war. Aware that she had to instill confidence and strength in her troops heading to battle—no easy feat for a woman leader, especially at a time when two unsuccessful female monarchs preceded her—her speech acknowledged her position as a woman but assured them she was as steadfast and strategic as a king. Here's an excerpt from what she said:

> *I know I have the body of a weak, feeble woman; but I have the heart and stomach of a king, and of a king of England too, and think foul scorn that Parma or Spain, or any prince of Europe, should dare to invade the borders of my realm; to which rather than any*

dishonor shall grow by me, I myself will take up arms, I myself will be your general, judge, and rewarder of every one of your virtues in the field . . . by your concord in the camp, and your valour in the field, we shall shortly have a famous victory over those enemies of my God, of my kingdom, and of my people.[9]

Many historians agree that Queen Elizabeth, who was also an accomplished poet, wrote the speech herself, as she knew exactly how to present herself to the public in a way that would resonate with her audience at that specific moment in time. Throughout her short speech, she speaks directly to her soldiers, without using ostentatious rhetoric, which the most authentic storytellers are skilled at. She began the address using "my lovely people" and expressed that she lives and would die for her kingdom: "live and die amongst you all" as a leader married to her people. She also evoked the nationalism that her troops desperately needed at the time, implying that the English had a direct connection to God that other nations don't have; "we shall shortly have a famous victory over those enemies of my God, of my kingdom, and of my people," she said. By the end of the speech, she established that she was far more than head of church and state—she was their general during the war and their savior. Ultimately, it was Queen Elizabeth's awareness of how she was perceived as a woman and what her people needed to hear at the moment that led to the power of that speech. And her physical appearance was as important as her words, which is why she dressed femininely, but fiercely prepared for war. The best storytellers don't kid themselves about who they are in the public eye—they're fully aware of how they're perceived and use their emotional intelligence to convey messages accordingly.

6. *Believe in what you're saying.* Hillary Clinton's 1995 speech at the United Nations Fourth World Conference on Women in Beijing marked a watershed moment for women's rights as well as for her political career.[10] "Human rights are women's rights, and women's

---

[9]Elizabeth Tilbury, "Elizabeth Tilbury's Speech," British Library, July 1588, www.bl.uk/learning/timeline/item102878.html.

[10]Amy Chozik, "Hillary Clinton's Beijing Speech on Women Resonates 20 Years Later," *New York Times*, September 5, 2015, https://www.nytimes.com/politics/first-draft/2015/09/05/20-years-later-hillary-clintons-beijing-speech-on-women-resonates/.

rights are human rights," were the defining words of a speech that conveyed that the issues facing women and girls are too often ignored or "silenced." Clinton referenced many tough issues women face globally, including dowry deaths (women who are murdered or driven to suicide due to husbands and in-laws attempting to extort women for larger dowries) and China's one-child policy. According to the *New York Times*, Clinton clashed with White House aides as well as the Chinese regime in preparing for the speech, as both urged her to dilute the remarks. Well before Clinton established herself as a political powerhouse in her own right, the White House "didn't think a first lady should dive into delicate diplomatic issues," according to the *Times*. Defying the wishes of her administration and upsetting Chinese leaders, Clinton spoke from the heart, and the speech gave her the global exposure she needed to set her up for a lifelong career in fighting for women's rights as a global figure. Her enduring words still carry the same weight they did 20 years ago, and her passion for making women's lives better carried across then (and it does now) because she truly believed in her message. If you're going to speak, make sure you're bullish about what you're going to say. When a storyteller is half-hearted—whether it's in a written piece, short film, speech, or any other form of communication—it's obvious to the audience and thereby far less compelling. As the adage goes, say what you mean and mean what you say; otherwise no one will care about your message.

7. *Be generous and empower your audience.* The best storytellers are generous. They don't hold back. They don't let their egos get in the way. Many times, they invite the audience in to share their stories, too. Because in the end, the audience is the hero that can effect change, not the storyteller. For ages, the most skilled storytellers have empowered listeners to take action. Each orator I've mentioned inspired the audience in some way to fight harder for equal rights, to have confidence in the leader, to feel less confused and scared about the state of the world, and, in Steve Jobs's case, to purchase an iPod. In all of these cases, the orators put the audience at the center of the story because they recognized the message was greater than the presenters themselves. As Harry Truman once said, "There is no limit to what you can accomplish as long as you don't care

who gets the credit for it." Sell your vision, and let the rest take care of itself. As strategic communicators, we have to do more than sell our company or its products if we truly want people to listen. We need to sell a big idea and activate our audience's imaginations, hopes, and aspirations. We need to make them feel, imagine what's possible, and encourage them to act. In every story you tell, create tension that builds to a captivating climax and then deliver a resolution. Ask yourself, after you've said what you need to say, what do you want your audience to do? Why should they care about what you have to say?

The best stories compel an action. If you're not compelling them to engage, interact, change their behavior, or see the world differently, go back to the drawing board.

As John Steinbeck said in *East of Eden*: "If a story is not about the hearer he will not listen. And here I made a rule—a great and interesting story is about everyone or it will not last."

So make it about human nature.

Insights

- Every form of storytelling, whether it's a portrait, film, political speech, a musical performance, a religious sermon, a novel, a documentary, or anything else, must be human in order to be great.

- The following principles will guide you to tell more human stories: Tailor your story for the situation and medium. Know when to speak. Prepare obsessively, but allow room for improvisation. Have self-awareness; know your audience and their mind-set. Have conviction in your beliefs. Be generous with the stories you tell—don't hold back—and seek to empower your audience.

Ask Yourself

- Are you connecting with your fans enough? Are you interacting with them in a human way?
- Do you consider your audience, the format, and message before you think about your brand?
- Is your work truly adding value to peoples' lives, or is it adding to the noise?

4

It's Life Stages, Not Ages: The Generation Myth and the Power of Personalization

The first step to being more human in our marketing and strategic communications efforts is to realize when we're making unhelpful assumptions about our customers. One of these is the myth that people are best defined by what generation they belong to.

Generations are an invention of demographers and have been eagerly adopted by journalists as an easy news peg to reach for in the rush for explanations.

But the explanations for human behavior, even mass behavior, are more nuanced than what year or decade we were born in.

A great deal of ink has been spilled recently about people born between 1981 and 1997, so-called millennials.

In truth, millennials aren't that different from other generations, aside from having higher student debt than their elders and growing up with smartphones, and it's a critical error to think of them as a homogenous, distinct group that we've never seen before.

Where did all these preconceived notions come from? Who decided that millennials are lazy, entitled, noncommittal and easily sidetracked by technology, or that baby boomers are technophobes who are set in their ways and don't care about future generations and just want to retire?

Years ago, psychologists believed that only bigoted people used stereotypes. But over time studies of unconscious bias revealed the truth that we all use stereotypes to categorize the social and physical world without even realizing it. And that ability to categorize and evaluate the world around us is central to our survival—it enables us to respond rapidly to situations because we may have had a similar experience before.

But in the world of marketing, where conscious choice and decision making are critical to success, stereotypes hold us back from understanding our audience enough to really reach them.

It's the same mistake pollsters make during elections, especially during the most recent U.S. presidential race and during the Brexit vote in the United Kingdom. Raw emotion, populism, anger, nationalism, class division, and other factors distorted accuracy in polling, ultimately putting pundits' flawed thinking on full display. A few weeks before the presidential election, a brilliant paper was published by researchers at Duke University that argued for many people, casting a vote has more to do with reinforcing a sense of self, perhaps as a progressive, a Christian, or a member of a minority community, than making a political decision based on policy preferences.[1] The researchers called for a new way to predict voter behavior by shifting emphasis from policy issues to voter identity.

Brands should have the same line of thinking in how they market to consumers. To rely on generational stereotypes (or stereotypes about people in general) to inform communication decisions is to invite trouble in the future. What marketers need to do is uncover individuals' real life stories to converse with them in a way that resonates rather than with generically manufactured messages, because age and traditional, basic markers of demographics will never determine a person's preferences and behaviors. Their life stage does.

The year I turned 38, it felt like my life was transformed overnight. I got married, bought a new house and a new car, and adopted a dog—all in a little over a month. My mind-set changed because I was entering a new phase—not because I turned 38. Some of my peers had done similar things when they turned 28. Some of them still haven't adopted a settled lifestyle that revolves around family, and they never will, a fact that makes them no less worthy of being understood by brands.

The changes in my life at 38 required new, welcomed commitments, responsibilities, and adaptations to my daily routine. For a long time, I had made my business commitments central to how I lived my life. Yet suddenly I had a family that became far more important than my work.

Most people have similar stories. It wasn't turning 18 that made them feel like an adult. It was purchasing a house, paying off debt, having a child, voting, or getting promoted. The expected progression of life stages isn't as linear as it was decades ago. The age range for having children and marrying is far broader than it used to be. People are changing careers and moving more often. Fewer people are buying homes.

---

[1] Libby Jenke and Scott A. Huette, "Issues or Identity? Cognitive Foundations of Voter Choice," *Trends in Cognitive Sciences* 20, no. 11 (November 2016): 794–804, www .cell.com/trends/cognitive-sciences/abstract/S1364-6613(16)30131-0.

So let's make sure "millennial," "baby boomer," "Gen Z," and all the other generational terms don't keep us from actually getting to know our audience. We owe it to ourselves to use all the analytical tools available to us today. Data offers us a more nuanced understanding of consumer mind-sets than we've ever had.

Knowing that a user is socially aware and health-conscious and understanding what causes she cares about changes how you'd approach that person, as would finding out that a female customer is a new mom and shops and thinks differently than she did a few years ago. Life stages are fluid and change seemingly overnight, and to be prepared, marketers need to constantly listen and remain nimble.

One way to listen that is available to any brand is to pay attention to what your users say on social media. The comments section of your hub, keywords on your social channels, data about what users do on their mobile phones or say in your surveys, what they buy or flag on a wish list, and when they're frustrated while trying to get customer support—these are all crucial sources of information.

When you aggregate that information, you can begin to put a face to the community your brand is convening. You begin to find out what they like, what they love, what angers them, and what they care about most.

Those details will suggest which personas you can use to plan out your brand interactions—2.0 versions, if you will, of generational stereotypes.

In other words, if you don't know who you're talking to, or worse, if you think you know who you're talking to, you're bound to say the wrong things.

Data and Privacy

The best way to get to know your customers is to collect data and analyze it with digital tools and a team of data scientists.

But before you do that, a few words of caution. The cloud of data that follows all of us through our lives is an invisible but necessary element to consider at the beginning of any decision that involves your customers.

Before you begin learning more about your customers, your team has to make many up-front decisions about how to collect the right data, communicate the practice to the customer and possibly offer opportunities to opt out, and, most important, establish safeguards to protect sensitive information.

These decisions can't be made in haste and must involve all major stakeholders. The data scientists, technologists, and IT security specialists on your IT team have to carefully weigh what information would be most valuable to know about customers, decide how they will use it to better serve the customer, ensure that proper security measures are in place before they start collecting, and plan how they would handle a potential breach after the fact because it is likely to happen. In 2015, the reported number of exposed identities jumped to an estimated half a billion, according to a report by Symantec.[2] Over the last few years, many companies have hired chief marketing technologists to align marketing technology with business goals, act as a liaison to IT, and evaluate and choose technology providers. They champion experimentation in technology for the sake of making the business more agile and customer-centric. They act as part strategist, part creative director, part technology leader, and part teacher. About half of chief marketing technologists are charged with helping craft new digital business models as well, according to *The Harvard Business Review.*[3]

Ongoing communication between marketers, IT, data scientists, developers, and others will be necessary as they work together to build new products and online destinations, and implement new tools that collect data. Breaches can result in steep fines, a lack of customer trust, and could even put the entire company at risk. So take the necessary steps to mitigate risks as much as possible, ensure that you're collecting the right information, and be transparent with customers about what you're doing.

---

[2]Matthew Reynold, "Half a Billion Identities Were Stolen or Exposed Online in 2015," *Wired,* April 12, 2016, www.wired.co.uk/article/identity-theft-symantec-security-2015-amount.
[3]Scott Brinker and Laura McLellan, "The Rise of the Chief Marketing Technologist," *Harvard Business Review,* July–August 2014, https://hbr.org/2014/07/the-rise-of-the-chief-marketing-technologist.

A study by Columbia Business School researchers, involving 8,000 people in the United States, Canada, the United Kingdom, France, and India, showed that the majority of people feel comfortable sharing their data if they trust the brand and are getting valuable data in return.[4] More than 75 percent said they were willing to share data with a brand they trust, and 80 percent said they would share nonrequired data for reward points, product recommendations, or for a tool to help them with complex decisions.

Consumers want to be able to decide what companies know about them; 86 percent want to exercise greater control over the data companies hold about them, and 85 percent want more information about the data companies collect. Cultivating trust by being fully transparent about practices and giving your customers the ability to opt in or out of data collection is the only way to navigate these waters. When executed with the consumer's trust, using data to create personalized experiences can work magic.

The Evolution of Personalization

In the mid-1990s, e-commerce websites such as Amazon and eBay began unveiling automated recommendation systems to offer users more personalized product recommendations based on a few criteria such as user feedback and ratings. Needless to say, recommendations weren't very good back then because of the few data points the systems took into account. At the time, similar systems were built for music streaming platforms to recommend music to users based on artists they had listened to, as well as a variation for movie recommendations that users could share over e-mail with a virtual community of movie fans.[5] Recommender systems quickly became popular, both in research and in commercial practice, and soon after computer science programs began offering entire courses on the subject.

---

[4]"What Is the Future of Data Sharing?," Columbia Business School, http://www8.gsb .columbia.edu/globalbrands/research/future-of-data-sharing, accessed January 31, 2017.
[5]Ben Schafer, Joseph A. Konstan, and John Riedl, "E-Commerce Recommendation Applications," Department of Computer Science and Engineering, University of Minnesota, http://files.grouplens.org/papers/ECRA.pdf, accessed February 1, 2017.

Over the last two decades, the scope of *recommender systems* has broadened immensely; while the term originally grew out of work in collaborative filtering (ratings from other users), it expanded to include á broader range of content-based and knowledge-based approaches, thanks to an ever-increasing amount of user data that can tell highly detailed stories about users, as well as smarter algorithms that can crunch it in real time.

Today, all kinds of websites use recommender systems with sophisticated algorithms that attempt to guess what we'll want, in most cases before we ourselves know we want it. Amazon, Netflix, Spotify, Tinder, Facebook, Stitcher, and many, many other platforms wouldn't have the customer and user base they have today if it weren't for personalization. Increasingly, personalization is becoming more baked into the user experience, and companies don't want you to be conscious that your experience is individual to you.

Netflix, for example, wants to present you with the shows and movies they think you're most likely to watch, but there's no "Recommended for you" messaging above any of their titles. Rather, the rows update regularly to reflect your viewing tastes as the company gets to know you. The recommendation engine is designed to shape your ambient environment in ways that won't interrupt your experience.

In the same way, dating platforms don't want you to know that they're paying attention to every swipe you make, noting your preference for certain attributes in a potential partner, such as race, as OkCupid founder Christian Rudder noted in his book *Dataclysm*. Sometimes, knowing just how much is being done to cater to your tastes can feel a bit creepy, but it isn't stopping companies like OkCupid and many of the other dating platforms from showing you the people they think you'd like. Like much of the physical infrastructure that caters to our needs, knowing some of the odd or boring details—like how sewage is processed or how traffic lights are optimized—doesn't stop us from enjoying the benefits.

Automated, seamless personalization is welcomed by millions of people who use the Internet. Google's Nest thermostat autonomously adjusts heating and cooling as it learns homeowners' habits. Among many of its individualized features and algorithmic recommendations based on user listening habits, Spotify's personalized Discover Weekly playlists have been particularly successful, garnering 6 billion to 7 billion streams[6] a little over a year after the feature debuted. And personalization in medicine is a true game changer; for example, smart insulin is a tiny embedded device for people with diabetes that pumps insulin into the blood when glucose is too high and then turns off when glucose returns to a safe level.

Personalization is disrupting just about every industry.

In the examples I've mentioned so far, automated personalization is not a problem for most people. But there are many cases where having users agree to a short, comprehensible terms of service agreement off the bat is crucial to building user trust and forestalling future problems.

An excellent example of opt-in data collection that provided value to customers is L'Oréal Paris's mobile apps, which features beauty diagnostic tools for skin care, face makeup, eye makeup, hair care, and hair color. Users must consent to terms and conditions prior to using the app. The Style My Hair, Makeup Genius, and Shade Genius apps allow users to upload photos of themselves and try different looks before they commit to purchasing products. These apps also ask users to fill out a short questionnaire to help them make recommendations. When users are near L'Oréal products in a store, they can scan the barcode and virtually try it in the moment to decide if they like it. The user can purchase products through the app as well. Dozens of other beauty companies, including Sephora, Aveda, and Yves Saint Laurent offer similar augmented reality consultation experiences that help the user make purchasing decisions. In L'Oréal's case, "the brand can extract over 148 unique data points per consumer, ranging from hair thickness and eye color to favorite lash looks and preferred foundation texture. In theory, the brand can segment consumers into more than 2.1 octillion highly granular personas, based on their diagnostic quiz results," according to

---

[6]Marty Swant, "Even Spotify Is Surprised by the Huge Success of Its Discover Weekly Playlists," *Adweek*, August 28, 2016, www.adweek.com/digital/even-spotify-surprised-huge-success-its-discover-weekly-playlists-173129/.

a report by digital intelligence research firm L2.[7] This level of granularity can help L'Oréal make better business decisions—informing the creation of new, improved products for its customers as well as helping the brand to decide which less popular products it will discontinue.

Another great example of personalization is Kohl's department stores' app, which works with an indoor positioning system that identifies exactly where shoppers are inside a store and offers them hyper-relevant content and coupons. As shoppers enter a Kohl's store, they receive a push notification that asks whether they want to opt in, and if they do, the app pushes lifestyle content—unbranded inspiration or advice such as a Pinterest board of looks for a living room or an article with home decor ideas while the shopper is in the home goods aisle. That data aggregates in real time with previously collected data Kohl's has about its shoppers' past purchases, which also factors into what content is served to users. Discounts and promotions are also sent to users' devices, but it's the lifestyle content that ensures an authentic connection between Kohl's and its customers—and ensures that users are getting something useful out of the experience, whether they purchase or not.

That data does more than boost customer loyalty, however. It can also help Kohl's decide how to best manage foot traffic throughout the store, and it might help store managers decide how they want to arrange product displays depending on where people linger in each aisle and what they end up purchasing.

Personalization for B2B

Business-to-business companies need personalization as much as business-to-consumer companies. What does that look like in practice? When the company knows who its buyers and users are and can see that they've bounced back and forth between several pages on their hub—let's say we're talking about an IT leader

---

[7]Marc Hummel, "The Crazy-Innovative Way L'Oréal Paris Captures Customer Data" Monetate Inc., July 28, 2015, www.monetate.com/blog/lessons-customer-data-capture-beauty-industry/.

reading up on cloud security on Dell's hub—the company can push a customized invitation for the user to check out solutions for his small or medium-sized business or a localized report on how a data center in the reader's area improved its security with Dell's solutions. Over e-mail, Dell can customize images, tone, wording, and the content itself for individual personas, so that an IT decision maker's e-mail looks different from a security-minded entrepreneur who wants to learn more.

Ultimately, personalization takes many forms, and I'm certain that we'll see many innovative approaches in the next few years. As futurist Kevin Kelly points out in his book *The Inevitable*, allowing your data out into the world in return for a personalized and much more useful experience in all the areas of life is a bargain we will all have to make to some degree. Very few people, Kelly predicts, will opt out of personalization entirely. It is a permanent dynamic in the way we do business and lead our lives.

Following are a few tactical areas of consideration for anybody building a website or designing a user experience to take into consideration. Even if you're not constructing an experience for your customers or readers, you can think about these factors the next time you are a customer or a reader yourself interacting with a brand. You may not have realized how much of your experience is designed to meet your interests.

DYNAMIC HOME PAGES

Many publishers struggle to find the balance between featuring user-specific, algorithmically recommended content prominently and allowing users to discover content on their own. There's also the question of whether to allow users to self-identify, so a page automatically populates with relevant content. Imagine a B2B financial investment company's hub, for example. An adviser would be looking for different content than an investor.

The best home pages on mobile and desktop lie somewhere in the middle, where personalized content is in an intuitive place on the page and is easy to find, but there's still room for users to explore and stumble upon new, interesting content that they might not have been searching for.

User experience should be a combination of art and science, with algorithms and an editor curating parts of the website. The human element is crucial, otherwise you end up with a situation like Facebook's at the end of 2016, where most of the algorithmically recommended content ended up confirming the political beliefs of the user, at the expense of truth and journalistic accuracy in some cases.

RECOMMENDING CONTENT TAKES EXPERIMENTATION AND HARD WORK

Netflix's data scientists calculated that users will spend just 60 to 90 seconds browsing before they get fed up and quit (and possibly switch to rival platforms, like Hulu or HBO GO). A typical user will review 10 to 20 titles, and perhaps three of those in any detail before they give up, according to research published in the journal *ACM Transactions on Management Information Systems.*

For that reason, it's essential that Netflix make extremely relevant recommendations in the first few rows of the interface. So the company made a serious investment in how it recommends content to users, hiring top data scientists and engineers to write a multitude of sophisticated algorithms that determine how to predict the rating that a member will give a video,[8] how to rank videos in each row,[9] and how to create meaningful groupings of videos.[10] Every detail of the user experience is carefully thought through, from the number of titles visible in each row, to parallax scroll navigation, to the clever names of groupings, such as "Watched by Claire Underwood," herself a character on Netflix's original series *House of Cards.* If you binge watched that show, odds are Claire's list showed up in your exploration of the site.

The overarching goal in all of this meticulous work is to enable users to discover content as quickly and easily as possible, so that

---

[8]"Netflix Prize," Netflix, www.netflixprize.com, accessed January 30, 2017.
[9]Xavier Amatriain and Justin Basilico, "Netflix Recommendations: Beyond the 5 Stars (Part 2)," Netflix, June 20, 2012, http://techblog.netflix.com/2012/06/netflix-recommendations-beyond-5-stars.html.
[10]Alexis C. Madrigal, "How Netflix Reverse Engineered Hollywood," *The Atlantic,* January 2, 2014, www.theatlantic.com/technology/archive/2014/01/how-netflix-reverse-engineered-hollywood/282679/.

they don't have to scroll through hundreds (and possibly thousands) of titles. For more than a decade, the streaming giant has been aiming to recommend content we want before we know we want it—an aspiration of nearly every publisher, social network, and mobile app.

The effort to make recommendations at the right time in a nonintrusive way is central to user engagement, whether it's at the bottom of a page with thumbnails as Vox.com does, or in a separate tab as Instagram (as of late 2016) does with its "Explore" tab. Hit explore and you'll see public photos from users you don't follow that you're likely to enjoy.

To create a stellar user experience and keep people using your website, app or service, experiment often through A/B testing and don't just follow what your competitors are doing.

PUSH RELEVANT CONTENT TO USERS, BUT NEVER TOO OFTEN

You want to push information to your users, but you never want to bombard them. Most users already receive a number of push notifications each day, from social media apps, e-mail, and text messages. So be mindful of what you're saying, the context of when you're saying it, and give them a clear shot to opt out.

Kohl's model of pushing contextually relevant lifestyle content to users works because it asks users for permission from the outset. Some publishers don't take Kohl's view of the matter and send along user data without asking users to opt in, which is ethically questionable.

When is the optimal time to send notifications, so that users won't feel annoyed and they'll want to experience your content?

This was a question researchers from Spain asked, which led them to develop a machine-learning model that they say can recognize when mobile phone users are bored. The technology automatically pushed content to those users so they would be more inclined to read it, according to Neiman Lab.[11]

---

[11]Laura Hazard Owen, "Soon, Publishers Will Be Able to Determine When Smartphones Users Are Bored and Push Content at Them," Nieman, September 2, 2015, www.niemanlab.org/2015/09/soon-publishers-will-be-able-to-determine-when-smartphone-users-are-bored-and-push-content-at-them/.

While users are more likely to read an article or watch a video when they have time for it, the practice can still feel intrusive, and there's an inherently false assumption that we always need to be occupied on our smartphones—what happened to introspection and down time? There's a place and time for push notifications—they can be especially helpful when you've got a meeting scheduled on your calendar and there's traffic on the road and Google Maps lets you know what time you should leave, for example. But tread lightly, because over 50 percent of app users find push notifications annoying, according to research by Localytics.[12]

LIMIT THE NUMBER OF E-MAILS YOU SEND, AND KEEP THEM PERSONAL

Among all the junk we receive on a daily basis over e-mail, only 21 percent of consumers say that they've received a memorable promotional e-mail in the past two months, according to a study by Litmus.[13]

The takeaway is that there's real opportunity to stand out when you've got something different and engaging to offer via e-mail. Spotify, for example, does a great job of sending personalized e-mails that you want to open and share, whether they're rewarding you for being a fan, occasionally notifying you of new singles from artists you listen to frequently, or sharing a "Year in Review" with data visualizations of your personal stats, such as how many hours you've listened in the past year and what your top artists and songs are. By integrating location data, Spotify even chooses to notify users when their favorite artists will be performing near them (as shown in Figure 4.1). Spotify doesn't send too many e-mails, and because all of them are relevant only to a particular individual's experience, you can see why users would consistently open them.

I love that Spotify shares the interesting data it collects about our behavior on the platform. At the bottom of its e-mails, it includes

---

[12]Caitlin O'Connell, "The Inside View: How Consumers Really Feel about Push Notifications," *Localytics*, January 20, 2016, http://info.localytics.com/blog/the-inside-view-how-consumers-really-feel-about-push-notifications.
[13]Chad White, "Creating Memorable Experiences [Infographic]," *Litmus*, September 28, 2015, https://litmus.com/blog/creating-memorable-shareworthy-email-experiences-infographic.

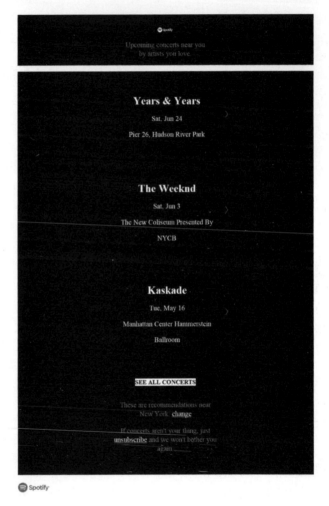

FIGURE 4.1   Personalized Spotify Email.

subtle calls to action that drive back to the platform such as, "Just For You, Discover music we think you'll love based on your listening history" with a link to your personal, algorithmically recommended weekly playlist.

These kinds of e-mails provide real value to users; each one is about the user as an individual, not about the brand itself. That's how you build brand affinity among your users. Ever since the beginning of direct mail, it's been a best practice to make all customer communications about the customer. Up until now, that was a matter of guesswork. With e-mails like these from Spotify, it's true in a new way.

APPROACH EACH SOCIAL PLATFORM WITH A DISTINCT STRATEGY

Brands should have unique strategies for paid and nonpaid social media posts. What's the difference? Paid posts allow you to craft messages targeted to specific audiences, and today it's easier than ever to home in on specific individuals on Facebook, Twitter, Instagram, and Snapchat by using paid targeting services based on each site's native capabilities. Meanwhile, nonpaid posts should be highly relatable and uniquely creative so that users are compelled to share it on their own.

Taco Bell is particularly adept at crafting posts that people will share. The company is consistently quirky, humorous, and over-the-top on social media, which is why its nonpaid posts often gain traction among fans. On Cinco de Mayo, Taco Bell featured a filter on Snapchat that made it possible for users to post selfies which turned their heads into a giant taco.

You could see how something like that would go viral. Business-to-consumer companies can create all kinds of fun filters like this to own specific moments in time.[14]

For business-to-business companies, LinkedIn and Facebook have a wealth of specific information on specific users and are therefore well suited for paid advertising. On LinkedIn, for example, businesses can filter users based on industry, companies they work for and have worked for, users with specific skills, groups they belong to, and causes they care about, among many other attributes. Before you go ahead and put money behind a campaign, the platform allows you to see how big your audience is. For example, you can tell how many people work in human resources in the United States or how many employees Wells Fargo has in Asia, to figure out how many people will see your messages and plan ahead. As a result, paid posts through LinkedIn can help you recruit,

[14]"15 Creative Snapchat Campaigns from Brands to Inspire Your Snap Strategy," Wallaroo Media, October 29, 2016, http://wallaroomedia.com/12-creative-snapchat-campaigns-from-brands-to-inspire-your-snap-strategy/.

promote awareness, and possibly even improve your image among people you really want to target.

Facebook's engine is also sophisticated, as it offers highly advanced ways for brands to target users beyond basic demographic information that people post about themselves in the "About Me" section. For example, brands can target users by life event through custom filters. When users change their locations and indicate they've moved, a furniture company can send targeted messages to that subset of people. When people indicate they're newly engaged, wedding photographers can push their services. You can layer other filters on top of these life events, such as specific user behaviors and a user's net worth for even greater granularity. And after Facebook knows who your customers are, there's a feature called Lookalike Audience that allows brands to reach prospects with similar attributes as your existing customers.

How does Facebook know so much about us? Like many social networks, the company has forged partnerships with data brokers such as Epsilon, Acxiom, and Datalogix to gain acuity from trillions of data transactions each year, which gives the social media network incredible insight into specific purchasing decisions that users don't share online.

To test Facebook's ability to personalize in such a specific way, one marketer who specializes in paid media pranked his roommate by sending highly personalized messages designed to make him paranoid.[15] Knowing that his roommate, who swallows swords for a living, has trouble swallowing pills, he created a Custom Audience campaign just for him with messages such as "Trouble swallowing pills? Does it seem ironic that swallowing swords is easy and then small pills make you gag?" causing the roommate to freak out over Facebook knowing way too much about him. He posted a screenshot of the ad saying that it was the "most targeted ad in the history of ad targeting."

It really works!

---

[15] Garett Sloane, "This Marketing Pro Practiced His Facebook Ad Targeting by Making His Roommate Completely Paranoid," *Adweek*, September 23, 2014, www.adweek .com/digital/roommate-makes-his-friend-paranoid-creepy-facebook-ads-160320/.

Mobile and Omnichannel Personalization

According to research by Responsys, 50 percent of people say the number one reason they download apps is to receive discounts and special offers.[16] And when that happens, they expect an entirely personalized experience with rewards and messages specific to their preferences. You've got far less screen real estate on mobile than on desktop, so your brand won't resonate with users unless every square centimeter of that space is used to cater to their needs.

But there are a few other reasons why mobile marketing is so powerful.

Mobile is the medium where you can really learn about your customers' behaviors and reach them in a way that's most effective. With mobile, you're able to see their location, the weather where they are, which screens they've viewed in how many sessions, when they've opened push and in-app messages, and—most crucially, when they've converted to a sale or when they finally said goodbye.

From a user experience standpoint, being able to see the path a user takes through a mobile site or app and then being able to combine it with relevant data allows marketers to deliver related content specific to the browsing patterns of users. For example, photo equipment retailer Jessops tracks movements and provides recommendations based on rules that limit the price difference between the product initially viewed and the final recommended product, as UXMag.com points out.[17]

Then there's the ability to gather data from other apps, which can lead to better contextual interactions. For example, if your clothing store's app has access to the user's calendar app, it can remind the user of a friend's upcoming birthday and can recommend buying a gift during the day when stores are open, and then it can show

---

[16]Heather MacKinnon, "Give Mobile Marketing a 'Push' [Infographic]," Oracle, February 5, 2014, https://blogs.oracle.com/marketingcloud/give-mobile-marketing-push-infographic.

[17]Stephen Powers Rogowski, "Contextualization Is the Key to Delivering Powerful, Personalized Digital Experiences," UXMagazine.com, March 11, 2013, https://uxmag.com/articles/contextualization-is-the-key-to-delivering-powerful-personalized-digital-experiences.

the user nearby store locations. Or, based on the user's location and weather, your app can feature products specific to the user's situation. Home Depot adjusts featured content for users based on seasonal changes, showing patio furniture to people in the South in early spring, while pitching kitchen-remodeling products to people in the still-chilly Northeast.

Once marketers have a strong mobile experience, they can aggregate the data and leverage it across different devices, creating specific experiences for each in a way that feels cohesive, rather than repetitive, for the user. If you know your user abandoned a shopping cart on a desktop and didn't complete the purchase, the brand can offer a deal when that user is near a store, or alert the person that the product is in stock and that she can try it on in person to see if she likes it. Conversely, if you're able to see that your user is browsing your store's products after seeing a targeted Instagram ad but ultimately doesn't purchase anything—as most of us don't (less than 30 percent of purchases came from mobile devices in 2015[18])—you can then retarget the individual on her desktop. In the future, all of our devices will work seamlessly together, with marketers operating within an ecosystem, dispersing the right messages at the right time in the right places. Creating a personalized mobile experience that measures user behavior and adapts in real time is the first step to that end.

Taking Personalization Off-Line

Once marketers have a keen understanding of who their users are and know how to speak to them, we can leverage for better individualized experiences off-line.

Brick-and-mortar shopping is still king, and it will be for years to come. E-commerce only accounts for 6.6 percent of all retail sales, and while it's rising—eMarketer analysts estimate that figure could become as much as 20 percent in the next 10 years[19]—it is unlikely

---

[18]Mark Brohan, "Mobile Commerce Is Now 30% of All U.S. E-Commerce," *Internet Retailer*, August 18, 2015, https://www.internetretailer.com/2015/08/18/mobile-commerce-now-30-all-us-e-commerce.

[19]Lucia Moses, "Data Points: Spending It," *Adweek*, April 18, 2012, www.adweek.com/brand-marketing/data-points-spending-it-139582/.

to ever replace in-person shopping. So it's crucial that marketers think about how to leverage all the knowledge they have about their customers when they're standing in front of them at checkout counters or when they're offering to help them in store.

Imagine a world in which Home Depot knows that you've recently bought a house and an in-store associate uses that information to tailor how he approaches and helps you. Or consider a situation where Gap knows you're about to enter the store, is aware you've got a certain pair of jeans on your online wish list, and a store employee checks to make sure your size is already on the shelf before you get to it.

There are few use cases like these so far, but marketers are starting to think about how they could use big data at every customer touch point, including when they're not online. Because at the end of the day, retailers that can tie together all of the data collected about a customer and adapt how they treat each individual stand a better chance at closing the deal.

As we move toward a customer-centric, outcomes-driven economy, total, data-driven experiences like this will become more common.

Some of these changes might seem unsettling now, but you can be sure that, as of this writing, retailers will be trying them out.

Insights

- Stop grouping your audiences only by age and location. Stereotypes hold us back from understanding our audiences enough to really reach them. So make a serious attempt to get to know them (with their permission, of course.)
- Before you begin learning more about your customers, your team has to make many up-front decisions about how to collect the right data, communicate the practice

(continued)

(continued)

to the customer and possibly offer opportunities to opt out, and, most importantly, establish safeguards to protect sensitive information.

♦ You can provide valuable experiences to your users and get to know them at the same time, and the majority of users are comfortable providing personal information in exchange for highly personalized experiences. There are several ways of doing that, including dynamic home pages, advanced algorithms, and push notifications with hyperrelevant content.

Ask Yourself

♦ What is your strategy for collecting data on users, and how do you tell them that you're doing it? Are you providing value in exchange for their information?

♦ What are you collecting, and is it useful to your company? If not all of it is useful, you need to rethink your approach.

♦ How do you plan to get more personalized in the coming years?

5

Atomize, Serialize, Magnetize, and Keep Your Velocity

Solving for Distribution

In the age of the educated consumer, every previous solution to a vital problem is now accompanied by a host of parallel solutions. In some ways, the growth of our problems is less worrisome than the need to keep up with the multiplicity of our solutions. Even if they all work, each solution demands a unique approach to execute. This means we have to be flexible and pivot quickly even in moments of certainty.

Education is one example. No part of the working population can rely, as it once did, on the sole solution of finite standardized education by age cohort to prepare it for a career. And at no point can education, including professional and vocational education, be said to be "completed" anymore. The gap between the rate of change and our collective institutional ability to cope with it, what Thomas Friedman calls our "physical technologies" and our "social technologies," is now too large for that to be the case.[1] For education to be relevant, it must be continuously refreshed.

All the traditional activities of education, like meeting in classrooms, doing homework, group work, and studying, are being arrayed in a host of new ways. Collaboration, while once limited to in-person meetings between students, can now happen asynchronously via the Internet. Startups like the Khan Academy are turning some basic assumptions on their heads—proposing for example that homework be done in groups during class while lectures be consumed in solitude at home online. Silicon Valley startups are now no longer valuing college degrees the same way they once did. Some see them as a liability rather than an asset. And educational reformers, like Ken Robinson,[2] are proposing that students of all ages enroll at whatever level they feel best serves their needs, not at the level that society has predetermined their learning trajectory.

In these shifting circumstances, publishers of educational materials are increasingly finding themselves in need of products optimized for whatever radical new solution to education comes along.

The same situation exists for every producer of content, including content marketers. The core questions are as tricky as ever to answer: how do you distribute your content once it's been produced? And what types of content is it wise to have on hand?

At SJR, we believe that even thinking of those as two separate questions is obsolete. The undecided factors of production and distribution feed into one another. The new solutions generated by each are part of a continuous, iterative process. How you produce content—how fast, in what length, and for what platforms—influences what content you produce and vice versa.

---

[1]Thomas Friedman, "Dancing in a Hurricane," *New York Times*, November 19, 2016.
[2]Ken Robinson, "Changing Education Paradigms," TED & RSA Animate, October 2010.

This means that the only lasting approaches to distribution are high-level, strategic ones, based on broad patterns of consumption and not specific platforms, the specifics of which change too frequently to come to any fixed conclusions about them. By the time you've figured out exactly how to game Twitter or Google's algorithm, for example, odds are they've changed it. And by the time I could've walked out onto the busy production floor of SJR and asked our strategists and editors what the best practices of the moment are, typed them up, and waited for them to appear in the print you are now reading, the content ecosystems of the Internet will inevitably have moved on.

That's why this section is called "Solving for Distribution" and not "The Distribution Solution." In the age of the educated consumer we have never solved. We are always solving.

Each of the following distribution strategies is a metaphor and offers guiding principles, not hard and fast rules. They are meant to be applied to the mechanics of specific platforms on a test-and-learn basis. During my years at SJR, I've always seen test-and-learn as our basic mode of operation, fitting for the skunkworks or experimental laboratory that we are.

But amidst all that churn, I have seen these four overarching patterns emerge as a way to make content that is not only original but widespread in its distribution and effective in its impact.

ATOMIZATION

Even a perfume's most precious ingredients, like musk or ambergris, which can sell for as much as $5,700 per pound,[3] are worthless unless they can be turned into a form that can be absorbed and enjoyed by the senses.

Ambergris is prized as a fixative in the world's finest perfumes. When added as an ingredient in the refining process, it not only adds its distinct aroma but allows the other notes in a perfume to last longer. When sprayed from the atomizing nozzle of a bottle, it settles

---

[3]"Ambergris Found on Anglesey Beach Sells for £11,000," BBC News, September 25, 2015, www.bbc.com/news/uk-wales-north-west-wales-34362556.

in fine particles in the air and on the body, spreading its delightful smell to the wearer and those around them.

But ambergris begins life as a greasy, lumpy substance in the intestines of whales. It was once extracted by whalers as part of the refining process that turned a whale's entire body into a number of different substances useful to humans, from lamp oil to braces for corsets. Ambergris is now sold only when it is found washed up on beaches in large, unsightly lumps—an extremely rare occurrence. Unless properly aged and refined, the odor of ambergris isn't especially pleasant.

The journey from unrefined but valuable substance to priceless atomized mist is a metaphor for one distribution strategy great content marketers can employ to get their brand's essential story out into the world in a way that permeates the media landscape.

SJR's name for this process is atomization and we define it this way, "the process of breaking down a narrative into individual pieces to widen reach and deepen the breadth of storytelling."

Imagine that the human resources department of a large company has recently implemented a new way of doing performance reviews.

It's a less labor intensive, faster, less formal way of getting good feedback to employees. The company finds the new process to be innovative, challenging, and enjoyable. And it's the perfect new piece in the company's evolving strategy to recruit millennials.

But the full story of the new process is a huge, unprocessed lump of information. It reaches deep into the company's institutional history and organizational structure, and its implementation is highly complex and still under way. Furthermore, there are a number of different angles the story could be told from and a number of different contenders to tell the story. To put the burden of all this on a single piece of content would be to produce something that would be impossible to consume in a single setting or risk being incoherent from the sheer number of ideas it attempts to link so closely together.

So, you atomize. You take a quote from an internal presentation and turn it into a tweet, then a graphically formatted quote for Instagram and Facebook. You take employee stories that reinforce the same talking point and put them up on Facebook. And, if the company is smart enough to have a content hub, you launch a series of videos and text pieces detailing different parts of the new process. You devise small, sharable pieces of content for every single platform where the company has a presence.

Like the whale's body, no part of your company's story ends up being wasted. And, like a fine perfume that emerges from the nozzle of an atomizer, your content is designed to spread far and wide in small pieces and delight wherever it goes.

Atomization works because of a fundamental truth about creating content for the web. Unlike every media ecosystem before it, the web has no center. Traditional advertising and PR campaigns were built on a hub and spoke model. The 30-second TV spot was most often the center or the hub, with radio spots, print ads, and other content extending out from it, referring to it, and directing attention back to it. In the time period when live TV occupied the undisputed center of global attention, this made excellent sense.

Now, attention is diffused. People still watch live TV, but they do it while paying attention to smaller screens at the same time. And people are just as likely to encounter part of your story for the first time in some unanticipated corner of the Internet as they are on your content hub or in a traditional media outlet.

As a strategy, atomization creates content that is capable of drifting into the web's many small communities and mobilizing them in pursuit of your brand.

SERIALIZATION

The American weight loss industry is worth about $60 billion per year, with over 5 million diet books sold, which together account for about half of all health and fitness books in the United States.[4] Magazines like *Men's Health* and *Self* have circulations well over 1.5 million (putting both comfortably in the top 50 U.S. magazines) with monthly issues promising accessible advice for losing weight

---

[4]Julia Belluz, "The Problem with Diet Books Written by Doctors," Vox.com, April 27, 2016, www.vox.com/2016/3/24/11296168/down-with-diet-books.

and getting healthy. It doesn't matter that, with small variations, the advice and the promised benefits are always essentially the same and have been the same for decades. Even the covers of each issue are nearly identical. In the United States, the appetite for dieting advice in its current form is at least a century old and shows no sign of ever being satisfied.

Why? Because weight loss outlets are masters of a powerful strategy that turns a few core ideas into an inexhaustible stream of fresh, original content worthy of readers' attention.

The term for it at SJR is *serialization*, and it has only become more essential in our digital communications landscape, where new content replaces old continuously.

Serialization is the art of targeting audiences with the same message repeatedly but in a way that still feels fresh. To be effective, a brand must have a clear sense of what it stands for. But to capture attention, brands must always be saying something new.

The word comes from the extended storylines that we follow on TV shows and, before them, that people read each week or month in magazines and newspapers. And the basic concept in all media is the same: Each time someone consumes serialized content, they are expecting something that's fundamentally the same, but just a little bit different to pique their interest.

Serialization is what makes medical dramas like *House* or police procedurals like *Law & Order* so successful. You probably don't quite remember what happens in each episode, but that's not the point. You remember the characters and what they stand for, the ongoing dynamics that make them interact with each other in such memorable ways. And you return to see the endless variations on the main themes.

Serialization is what stories look like when they become regular parts of our lives. As a vehicle for the dissemination of brands, serialization is invaluable.

One of the entertainment world's most enduring characters, Sherlock Holmes, came into being because of the commercial possibilities of serialization. When he was created by Sir Arthur

Conan Doyle in the late 1800s, Holmes was already one of many fictional detectives. Doyle's great style and knack for evoking a sense of mystery set Holmes apart, but it was Doyle's content strategy that made his detective immortal.

The traditional way to serialize novels had been to take a long, continuous story and simply split it up into small parts. If you picked up an issue of a magazine or newspaper that was serializing a novel, and you hadn't read the previous chapters, then you were out of luck. The many beloved novels of Charles Dickens and even Tolstoy's *War & Peace* were published this way. They would unspool in the public consciousness over several years, but had beginnings, middles, and ends.

But Doyle designed his serialized stories as self-contained units. At the start of each story, he made a point, with just a few quick strokes of the pen, of informing you that Holmes was an eccentric genius, Watson his affable companion, and that there was a mystery to be solved. For repeat readers, there was the comfort of a recurring formula: A mysterious man or woman visits 221B Baker Street, Holmes deduces something impossible from small clues about their appearance, and then the real story begins. And for first-time readers, they had everything they needed to join in the fun.

Through repeated exposure, Holmes took on the stature of a real person in the mind of the public, so much so that Conan Doyle had trouble killing him off and, long after he grew tired of writing Holmes stories, was essentially bullied into writing more of them by an adoring public.

More than any other content strategy, serialization is what has the potential to generate true bonds of affection between a brand and an audience. Anything that is a ritual has the possibility of becoming beloved.

MAGNETIZATION

Despite having no recognizable center, the web has self-organized into a loose network of communities based on affinity. Facebook, Twitter, and Instagram are best classified as platforms not communities. They each have users numbering in the billions or millions.

But within them and in the open Internet outside their walls, true communities have coalesced.

Author Steven Johnson has compared these communities to the densely settled hill towns in Italy during the Renaissance, which had a population neither too small to contain real intellectual diversity and brainpower nor too large to prevent the growth of useful connections between people and groups that were developing new ideas and ways of doing business.[5] The result of the loose network of these communities across Italy in the fourteenth and fifteenth centuries was the massive boost in human processing power that jump-started the world into a new era of technological and economic growth.

On a macro level, the same thing seems to be happening at this moment in history, but globally and powered by the communities of the web instead. Most remarkably, this process doesn't seem to be happening by chance, as it did in previous centuries. While it's not possible to fully engineer the growth of these communities, it is possible to plant the seedlings for them in the form of engaging pieces of content.

Game designer and futurist Jane McGonigal describes one such moment that happened in the wake of the attacks of September 11th. She had been a member of the tight-knit group of players of an online game called *The Beast*. The game was a collaborative murder mystery that played out over a series of fake websites scattered across the web. The entire game was created by Microsoft in cooperation with Warner Brothers as a piece of promotional content for the 2001 Steven Spielberg film, *A.I.* The game is still celebrated as one of the founding moments of the alternate reality gaming genre, and it was so successful that it outlived the theatrical run of the film. Most remarkable to McGonigal was what happened to the user base after the game ended. When the twin towers in New York City were attacked, *The Beast*'s user forums reactivated and filled up again with gamers who were no longer seeking to solve the puzzles in the game but the urgent, real-world mystery of how the attack had happened. The players also activated their network to coordinate relief efforts.

[5]Steven Berlin Johnson, "The Amazing Power of Networks," CNN.com, October 3, 2010.

What began as behavior seeded by a piece of content marketing spilled over into the evolution of a real-world community with real-world goals and impact.[6] The event was pivotal in McGonigal's career; to this day her research is focused on the latent power of computer games to change the real world.

When users gather around a piece of content and then activate together for a common purpose, SJR calls it *magnetization*. It is similar to the response that a traditional direct marketing campaign might receive but different in an important way. *Magnetization* is a natural, loosely suggested response, not one directly suggested by any messages in the content.

Just as a pile of iron filings is drawn to a magnet, users are naturally drawn toward content that takes risks and expresses an opinion, and when they are moved by what they see and read they have a tendency to move together in real ways.

Magnetization is one of the key differences between traditional advertising or public relations and content marketing. Both can spur groups of people to action, but only content marketing creates communities that can be mobilized more than once and, much more important, that mobilize themselves. With every piece of content you release into the world, you create another convening point for potential action.

KEEPING YOUR VELOCITY

The future belongs to those who can maintain their velocity.

It is a fact that the pace of life is accelerating. And it is fundamentally altering the formulation of strategy in all areas of human life, from warfare to business to communications.

Up until the late 1990s, a good book about strategic communications from, say, 1920 would have the same essential advice as one published in 1990. But with the Internet, speed, always a crucial advantage, has become *the* crucial advantage.

---

[6]Jane McGonigal, "How to Think (And Learn) Like a Futurist," keynote address at SXSWedu 2016 in Austin, Texas, https://www.youtube.com/watch?v=CKvMmtclUBA.

Much has been made of Moore's law, which correctly predicted in 1970 that computers would double their speed and power about every two years. But less has been made of the effect that this exponential rate of change is exerting on every facet of life. Everything that depends, even to a small degree, on digital technology has also become faster.

Because of digital data analysis, the number of planets discovered outside our own solar system has jumped from just a handful a year in 2000 to more than 900 in 2014.[7] Since 2009, the average financial transaction is 50 percent faster, dropping from 16 milliseconds to 8.1 milliseconds.[8] Since the 1930s, average shot length in movies has been compressed from 12.5 seconds to 2.5 seconds.[9] In 2015, the average American checked his phone 46 times a day, up from 33 times in 2013. If you're a millennial, that number jumps to about 74 times per day.[10] In every field, the rate at which we make new technology has accelerated, and that technology has, in turn, accelerated us.

The ways we shop, collaborate, learn, and make decisions have all gotten faster. Our effects on the environment, our institutions, and the people around us—all of it—have gotten faster.

This has stripped away a persistent belief that all organizations harbor—the belief that there is time. Time to fully understand the task at hand. Time to build the perfect product. Time to craft the perfect communications strategy.

There is now objectively less time for all of these tasks than at any moment in human history. And by the time you are done reading this page, there will be even less. The ability to shape the future belongs solely to those who can maintain their velocity no matter what.

---

[7]Digital Press Kit - Kepler Planet Bonanza, NASA, February 26, 2014, https://www.nasa.gov/ames/kepler/digital-press-kit-kepler-planet-bonanza.

[8]"High Frequency Trading Decoded," The Alert Investor by Financial Industry Regulatory Agency, June 26, 2015, https://www.thealertinvestor.com/high-frequency-trading-decoded-infographic/.

[9]Greg Miller, "Data from a Century of Cinema Reveals How Movies Have Evolved," September 8, 2014, https://www.wired.com/2014/09/cinema-is-evolving/.

[10]Lia Eadiccio, "Americans Check Their Phones 8 Billion Times a Day," December 15, 2015, http://time.com/4147614/smartphone-usage-us-2015/.

At SJR, we say "velocity" rather than speed to highlight an important difference. Any object moving through space can have speed. It's only when you move through space with both speed and purpose that you have velocity as we deem it.

Velocity implies speed, but also precision, and above all, purpose, all at the same time.

Everybody knows that it is great to be first to market. But knowing what to do once you get to market is even better.

Velocity Is Transformational

As Eric Ries, author of *The Lean Startup*, puts it, there is a persistent belief, endemic either to U.S. capitalism or possibly human nature, that by spending just a bit more time and a bit more money, it is possible to protect our endeavors and by extension ourselves from future harm.

This belief, Ries says, is not only blind but promotes blindness. It is only through the process of trial and error, or, on a grander scale, failure, that we are capable of learning.[11]

The perennial slowdown that comes from wanting certainty is what eventually leads to the cementing of hierarchies and bureaucracies, the overgrowth of formal communications within a company, and the slow overspecialization of individual jobs.

The process of violent revolution or institutional collapse is the intrusion into this state of affairs of urgent, unmet needs. In our accelerated age, we don't have time for either. And velocity is an engine for avoiding these twin upsets.

Velocity, when applied to content marketing, can be an engine for continuous renewal, because maintaining velocity forces us to move forward without all the answers.

In Ries' philosophy, which is designed to accelerate the creation and launch of digital and physical products, that engine is called the MVP, or minimum viable product. It is the simplest form of your

---

[11]Eric Ries, panel discussion on *The Lean Startup*, Cambridge, MA, June 7, 2016.

product that successfully meets the needs of the market. It is both effective and necessarily imperfect, and how consumers respond to it shapes the future of your business and your product. The MVP is designed to get you moving and learning at the same time.

SJR takes a similar approach to the creation of content. We believe that if you're not releasing your product with a few bugs, you're almost certainly waiting too long.

For large, legacy companies, this can be a serious challenge but also an incredible opportunity to change.

Scratch the surface of the most imposing, iconic corporate brand, and you are quite likely to find a culture that demands approval and buy in from every disparate part of the organization and every link in the chain of command before it is deemed ready for public consumption.

But by the time this has happened, your product—the piece of content—is not only drained of all coherence and originality, it has been rendered irrelevant by the passing on of attention, from both the public and your own employees, to other issues.

This is not a hypothetical scenario I am building up just to take down. At SJR, we've seen communications as short as a single tweet travel through multiple layers of approval before arriving on the web hours, days, or even weeks after the event it refers to. Scenarios like that represent a misunderstanding of the centrality of speed in a digital world, and also a missed opportunity to shape the conversation sooner, possibly first.

In a news cycle that can be measured in a number of hours, such a failure to move can actually be catastrophic. As the great psychologist Carl Jung said, "The world will ask who you are, and if you do not respond, it will tell you." At best, the response of the Internet to new information about a brand is impossible to predict. At worst, it is destructive.

Velocity is a broom that sweeps all of this away. As the bringer of speed, digital technology in all its forms is corrosive of hierarchy and overspecialization. It is the enemy of unnecessary formality and bureaucracy. And it has a magical ability to shake up a company and reveal where its treasure (its native sources of wonder, wisdom, and delight—see Chapter 1) is buried. Speed is not only preventative but transformational.

Crisis communications are an instructive example. In the wake of the unthinkable—an oil spill, a lethal product failure, bankruptcy, or scandal—speed above all else is forced on a brand. When the world's attention is turned on you, every moment that passes without a response is one in which the world is busy creating its own narrative about you, and without you.

All good crisis responses have the same characteristics. They are swift, transparent, sincere, and sincerely focused on getting beneficial information to consumers as quickly as possible. To deviate from any of these characteristics, as fear and excessive caution move us to do almost every time, is to court disaster.

To embrace all of them not only gives your brand its surest chances of survival, but also—and this is a fact often overlooked—to transform your company for the better.

Brands are not unlike people. If they can emerge from crisis intact, they are stronger and more knowledgeable than they were before, something they can carry with them throughout their lives.

On the other side of a successful crisis communication is a more educated public, a transformed company, and, in some cases, a transformed world.

Companies that survive brand-level existential threats tend to have the following changes: a more proactive public affairs department, a better focus on swift and transparent internal communications, a direct relationship between the executive leadership and the public, and overall muscle for the swift, decisive response to any threat.

Embracing SJR's conception of velocity builds this muscle without the need for crisis.

Insights

- In our age of continuous change, we have never solved the problem of distribution, but we must always be solving for it.
- The Internet has no central distribution hub, so to make your content capable of being everywhere, you atomize it.
- People demand fresh content continuously, but your brand can (and should) only stand for a few things. The solution? Serialize your content.

Ask Yourself

- Even if I have content out there, am I creating it fast enough to shape the narrative rather than letting other do it for me?
- Am I creating communities that will take action around my brand, or am I just capturing fleeting moments of attention?
- What stories in my company seem too long to tell but might be offered to the world as serialized or atomized content?

6

Only Connect: Creativity and Consistency

Only connect! That was the whole of her sermon. Only connect the prose and the passion, and both will be exalted, and human love will be seen at its height. Live in fragments no longer.

—E. M. Forster

The great challenge for organizations and the individuals who comprise them is to come up with sufficient creativity to solve their problems and those of their clients. When viewed from the perspective of an entire organization, creativity becomes, essentially, a supply and demand problem, as unromantic as the need for the raw materials that make up the goods in a factory.

The paradox is that as the world becomes faster and more connected, this supply and demand problem becomes tougher and tougher to solve. As each link in the chain of all our interconnected systems—infrastructure, health care, finance, client services, media—becomes stronger, the weaker links have to get stronger. Standards that may have supported society 50, 20, or even just 10 years ago are no longer good enough. Economist David Autor expressed this idea in a TEDx talk in 2016, and used it to help explain why, despite a century and a quarter of continued automation, the proportion of people with jobs has always gone up.

So how do we solve the supply and demand problem of creativity for ourselves and our institutions?

It's hard to cut through the noise of everyday life and develop our best ideas when we're constantly distracted by a stream of information and stimuli. For creatives, technology enables collaborative processes and sparks inspiration, but the widespread accessibility of information and our growing dependency on digital tools can also discourage divergent thinking. When it's easy to see what everyone else is doing, it can be harder to come up with novel ideas.

For individuals, inventive ideas come from conversations with other people as well as in moments of complete solitude. For companies, creativity comes from a mixture of conditions as well as from allowing a constant flow of new ideas and people. Most important of all is creating a culture where people can make authentic connections with one another.

Companies that strive to have the best ideas first need to build a complete, holistic culture of creativity. Here are some places to start.

Building a Content Culture

Every company is built by humans who come together each day in pursuit of a shared objective. Businesses express a vision through company values and mission statements with the hope that both will permeate all corners of an organization. Having a clearly stated mission defines the company's identity and can bring people across departments together.

In the same way, a strong content marketing program, in which the brand has a clearly defined voice, set of goals, and the will to stay true to its identity, can unify an organization. The most successful content programs have buy in from across the organization, especially from the top. And they can give employees a clear understanding of how their day-to-day tasks ladder up to the larger business goals of the company.

Unless your company is in a heavily regulated industry, where there are restraints to what your brand can say, allowing creatives to take ownership of their projects will allow them to bring unmatched energy and imagination to their work that, well, most brands lack. Once the right people are on board with a shared vision, leadership should take a step back. Provide support when needed, but allow your creators to work independently. The results will surprise you.

When employees are able to be creative within a framework, the content becomes a reflection of the organization's company culture. It shines through in writing, design, social posts, and videos. These personal touches of each individual are the mark of truly original content. It makes the brand one of a kind, which is what your customers want. Collectively, these personal touches are what set you apart from your competitors.

A business is a set of structures, but it's also a collection of minds, personalities, and attitudes. Content is a method by which the sum of individuals makes up the brand's identity. When you have a diverse group of people with a range of talents and areas of expertise working together to tell the brand's story, it's an expression of the brand's culture—a more genuine way of communicating compared to how it happened years ago, when press releases were the primary method for external communications and PR departments were gatekeepers.

In the nascent stages of the digital transformation, public relations departments at corporations were adept at sharing messages but they didn't understand emerging social platforms. Meanwhile, marketers quickly adopted new digital tools but struggled with messaging. Today, these departments are interdependent and reliant on many other groups across the company. It's simply impossible to tell your best stories effectively in silos.

At companies where there's a culture for content marketing, there's a transfer of knowledge happening between people with years of industry expertise and storytellers—nuggets of gold that were once buried are being extracted and prized. This collaboration is the best way to authentically connect with other people and liberate the knowledge within your company that's dying to get out.

It all starts with hiring curious people who think outside the box and are passionate about your brand.

The best teams come from diverse backgrounds. Former journalists are obvious hires for many content studios and brands, because they bring objectivity, strong editorial judgment, specific expertise, and speed to their work. But consider screenwriters, fiction writers, and bloggers as well.

On the video team, consider the former reality television producer as well as the documentary filmmaker and the former news producer. The applicant for the illustrator role, who majored in ceramics at art school but has an incredible Tumblr filled with her work—hire her. The most talented people I've met in this industry have come from the most unexpected places. You want to hire doers, makers, and collaborators who can inspire others and aren't afraid of hard work. Not much else should matter beyond that. It's diversity that drives innovation.

After you've got your people in place, empower them to pursue projects they're most interested in with people from different teams. At SJR and many other content agencies, regular brainstorms help us come up with our best ideas. With people from editorial, video, design, account management, and social in the same room from the start, we're able to conceptualize big-picture ideas for clients as well as plot the logistics and feasibility of a project. We also ask our clients to help us dig, so we'll meet with various teams and subject matter experts to hunt for interesting story angles.

A collaborative approach to storytelling puts everyone on an even playing field, regardless of title or years in the industry. Today's content creators—both inside corporations and at agencies—operate as startups do, with speed and a lack of hierarchical roadblocks. It gives creatives the freedom to do their best work.

To be a successful storyteller, you have to have the mind-set that everything is interesting—you just have to search for the unexpected angle.

As author Nicholson Baker eloquently said in the *New York Times*:

> You have to poke at a thing, sometimes, and find out where it squeaks. Any seemingly dull thing is made up of subsidiary things. It's a composite—of smaller events or decisions. Or of atoms and molecules and prejudices and hunches that are fireflying around in unexpected and impossible trajectories. Everything is interesting because everything is not what it is, but is something on the way to being something else. Everything has a history and a secret stash of fascination.[1]

Art can be scrutinized in hundreds of ways. The only thing you can be sure of about how people will perceive art is that their perceptions will differ. Consensus will never be reached. At brands, not reaching a consensus on a piece of work prevents it from seeing the light of day.

When too many different stakeholders are involved, it might feel tempting to rewrite a blog post or delete it entirely. Or you might ditch a piece of design because the font and colors just feel off. Resist the temptation. Don't doubt yourself. Especially at the start, overediting

---

[1]Nicholson Baker, "Fortress of Tedium: What I Learned as a Substitute Teacher," *New York Times*, September 7, 2016, https://www.nytimes.com/2016/09/11/magazine/fortress-of-tedium-what-i-learned-as-a-substitute-teacher.html?_r=1.

takes away the storyteller's unique voice. The personal touch disappears. High standards are important but so is trusting the creative judgment of the people you've hired.

As your people tell stories, it's important to remember that there's no such thing as perfect in creative work. Embrace it. Imperfection is what makes creations human and ultimately meaningful to the user. Publishing consistently, with authentic stories that provide value to the reader the same way service journalism does, matters more than striving for unattainable perfectionism.

When you discourage perfection, you encourage experimentation, and that's a major culture booster. Open-mindedness, curiosity, and diverse perspectives lead to more creative work. Incentivize and reward it as much as possible.

Inspiring Organization-wide Creativity

Culture and creativity go hand in hand. Many times, especially at corporations with a lot of hierarchy, the absence of creative ideas isn't because your employees aren't creative people. It's because your employees aren't encouraged to bring their ideas to the surface. The bottleneck starts at the top.

Google's founders, for example, tracked the progress of ideas that upper management had backed as opposed to ideas that had been executed without support from higher-ups. They found that employees' autonomy and success went hand in hand.[2]

Solve that by creating an atmosphere of trust, in which employees of all skill levels, including interns, are encouraged to bring forth big ideas, even if they aren't fully fleshed out. Then embolden them to bring ideas to colleagues, rather than upper-level management. If you have the right people in place, there won't be widespread anarchy—there will be uninterrupted invention.

---

[2]Teresa Amabile and Mukti Khaire, "Creativity and the Role of the Leader," *Harvard Business Review*, October 2008, https://hbr.org/2008/10/creativity-and-the-role-of-the-leader.

Don't forget to reward teamwork as often as you reward individual innovation, perhaps by tying a percentage of employees' bonuses to how well they work with others. Find a way to make collaboration a metric for success, and measure it using analytics tools as Intuit does when it tracks where new product ideas come from and how they improved business outcomes.[3]

Innovation should come from collaboration outside your company's walls as well. The Wright brothers didn't build and recognize the commercial success of the airplane on their own. The aviation enthusiasts openly discussed their developments with other hobbyists and built upon others' discoveries. There's a reason why open source software is so innovative; collaboration overcomes technical challenges and advances progress in a way that individuals most often cannot. This revered depiction we have of Steve Jobs as a lone genius who invented the iPhone all on his own couldn't be farther from the truth. Jobs would have never been able to build it by himself—he needed feedback from people inside and outside of his company to find the best path forward.

It's foolish to view people from outside your company only as competitors. You certainly don't want to share proprietary trade secrets with everyone, but there is so much value in collaborating outside of your company, and leaders don't encourage it enough. In the early days of SJR, a lot of my time went toward building a massive network, because I knew I would fail fast if I expected the company to succeed as an island unto itself.

Like the ever-evolving technology industry, content marketing is in its nascent stages. The only way we're going to get better at telling stories is by learning from each other's failures. Running into difficulties building a virtual reality app? Connect with other developers. Unsure how your client might react to a proposed campaign? Ask a sister agency for a second opinion. It doesn't make your team appear

---

[3]L. D. DeSimone, George N. Hatsopoulos, William F. O'Brien, Bill Harris, and Charles P. Holt, "How Can Big Companies Keep the Entrepreneurial Spirit Alive?" *Harvard Business Review*, November–December 1995, https://hbr.org/1995/11/how-can-big-companies-keep-the-entrepreneurial-spirit-alive.

weak when you ask for help—we all need it sometimes. It's time we problem solve together.

As much as I'm an advocate for collaboration, there's research we can't ignore around how individuals have their most creative moments.

Individual Creativity

There's plenty of research around how employees can unleash inner creativity. Meditation, exercising, walking through nature, and travelling somewhere new are just a few recommendations.

Inspiration often strikes when we least expect it, at moments when we aren't trying hard to be creative. It might take hours, even months of diligent practice, research, mental preparation, and trial and error, but when it comes down to the wire, we get the best from ourselves by relaxing and trusting in our abilities. Chinese philosophers, from Confucius to Lao Tzu, called this state of mind *wu-wei*, and it means "try-not-try."

Your physical workspace is just as important as your headspace, though.

Today's employers have torn down cubicles, walls, and corner offices in exchange for open office floor plans to encourage a more democratic way of working that increases the exchange of information as well as camaraderie. Privacy is a luxury that few have access to. According to the *New York Times*, roughly 70 percent of office workers inhabit open floor plans, and the average amount of space allotted to each employee shrank 300 square feet, from 500 square feet in the 1970s to 200 square feet in 2010.[4]

Open offices are great for collaboration, but they can stifle creativity. When solving logistical problems, a certain amount of friction and random interaction is crucial. But those workers who

---

[4]Susan Cain, "The Rise of the New Groupthink," *The New York Times*. January 13, 2012, www.nytimes.com/2012/01/15/opinion/sunday/the-rise-of-the-new-groupthink.html.

are doing your deep thinking for you need permission to go off on uninterrupted journeys of discovery and intense, solitary work. These journeys sometimes last a few hours and sometimes a few days. The important thing is to let your team members know that they're allowed to go on them.

And psychologists have determined that many extraordinarily creative people have preferred to do their most important work alone, including Sir Isaac Newton, Pablo Picasso, J. K. Rowling, and Frederic Chopin.

What does this mean for the worker? Private time is equally as important as brainstorming, and if your office doesn't have enough private rooms, it's essential that you allow your employees the flexibility to work from anywhere. Some people need white walls and a grey carpet to avoid distractions. Some people need to have their desk face a window. Others need to have their desk face a wall.

When SJR moved into a bigger office, we built many private rooms into our floor plan. And we allow people to do some of their work from home.

We can hack our creative processes by figuring out when we're most "up"—if you work best at 5 A.M., then get up and do it. If you find that you get a daily burst of inspiration right when you should be going to bed, gather your tools and stay up late. If your habits mean going to bed at 9 P.M. or 9 A.M., so be it. Especially in the age of digital collaboration, it doesn't matter that we show up to the same office from 9 to 5. You're worth more to your company if you can produce a regular stream of work. It's up to you to let others know how to make that happen, and then stick to it.

Some creative people tend to have certain personality traits: unconventionality, curiosity, openness to experiences and one's inner life, tolerance for disarray and complexity, high emotional intelligence, and confidence to express themselves without fear of judgment are a few. Some of us are born more creative than others; the brain works differently for everybody. Creative people aren't "right brained," rather, neurologists have determined they use many regions inside the frontal, parietal, and temporal lobes of the brain at once.[5] And researchers at Cornell University found that creative people have smaller corpus callosums, the nerve bundles that connect the left and right hemispheres of the brain.[6] To an extent, creativity is not malleable. But it can be nurtured. Here's how you can coach employees to be more creative:

- Provide feedback as much as possible. In a study with 456 supervisors and employees, researchers found that employees given feedback perform more creatively than their counterparts.

- Challenge people with projects they love. Pretty obvious, right? Well, science backs it up, too—employees who are intrinsically motivated by projects they enjoy and that interest them often come up with more creative solutions. Meanwhile, research shows that extrinsic motivators, such as financial incentives, do not inspire greater creativity.[7]

- Foster your employees' expertise in areas they're passionate about. Without a highly relevant skill set or knowledge of a specific area, they won't be able to improvise. So give them opportunities to learn; offer to pay for design classes for your designers, or send your writers to writing workshops.

- Remind your team that at the start of the creative process, a mixture of ideas will come to mind, both good and bad. The trick is to avoid too much judgment, keep moving, exploring, and experimenting until you find the next thing that fascinates you. For those of us whose careers demand creativity, we have no choice but to be like sharks—in constant motion.

---

[5]Carolyn Gregoire, and Scott Barry Kaufman, "Creative People's Brains Really Do Work Differently," *Quartz*, January 4, 2016, https://qz.com/584850/creative-peoples-brains-really-do-work-differently/.

[6]D. W. Moore, R. A. Bhadelia, R. L. Billings, C. Fulwiller, K. M. Heilman, K. M. Rood, and D. A. Gansler, "Hemispheric Connectivity and the Visual-Spatial Divergent-Thinking Component of Creativity," *Brain and Cognition* 70, no. 3 (August 2009): 267–272, https://www.ncbi.nlm.nih.gov/pubmed/19356836.

[7]Katleen E. M. de Stobbeleir, Susan J. Ashford, and Dirk Buyens, "Self-Regulation of Creativity at Work: The Role of Feedback-Seeking Behavior in Creative Performance," Academy of Management, August 1, 2011, http://amj.aom.org/content/54/4/811.short.

- Encourage them to take risks that could end in failure.
  As philosopher Daniel Dennett has said, "The chief trick to
  making good mistakes is not to hide them—especially not from
  yourself." The prospect of failure is terrifying; no one wants to
  feel vulnerable, but the potential for growth is enormous.
  If you're looking to do truly innovative work, you can't plot all
  your moves before you make them. You have to embrace the
  possibility of failure and openly explore how to learn from it.
  "We must think of the cost of failure as an investment in the
  future," Pixar co-founder Ed Catmull says.

PRACTICAL IDEAS FOR SPARKING CREATIVITY

- *15-minute creative retreats*: Staying creative doesn't have to
  mean hours of looking for inspiration. Fifteen minutes is
  sometimes all you need to get into a new frame of mind. A nap.
  A browse through an art book. A walk around the block. Free
  writing. Free drawing. Listening to music and staring at the
  wall. Even playing a quick game of tic-tac-toe. The only
  requirement is to get your eyes off of whatever you've been
  looking at, be it a screen, the wall of conference room, or the
  page of a notebook. Your brain is like any other organ. It needs
  variety to avoid repetitive stress injury and fatigue. Here are
  some 15-minute creativity boosts:
  - *Overdo it*. Overwrite. Overact. Overreact. Use a color that's
    too bright, a phrase that's too flowery, or a pitch that's too
    aggressive. Tell a bad joke. Design the worst slide for a
    presentation. Write a paragraph that's too serious or too
    absurd. You can always walk it back, tone it down, or make it
    better. But you might just find that you don't need to.
  - *Steal*. What path lead you to this moment of creative pressure?
    Why aren't you an accountant or a lawyer or a banker? It's
    likely because at some point in the past you were inspired by
    the work of a creative person. Something visual, like a
    sculpture, a painting, or a film. Or something made out of
    words. Go back to the last thing that inspired you and imitate
    it. Pick a subject that's your own and try to do something in the
    same style. Chances are, nobody will notice your theft—and
    you'll get unstuck and learn something in the process.

- *Strand yourself.* Sometimes the best aid to creativity isn't inspiration. It's boredom. Turn off your phone. Shut down your computer. Turn off the Wi-Fi if necessary. Go somewhere where you won't be interrupted or distracted and where you won't be tempted to interrupt or distract anybody else. Spend 15 minutes without external input, and write down whatever thoughts come to you.

- *Cut ups.* Get a pair of scissors and some old magazines and newspapers. Cut out images and words that look interesting. There need not be any rational connection between them, and you don't need to spend forever doing this. Ten images or phrases is enough. Put your clippings into a hat, a bag, or just toss them up into the air. Take out the first three that fall at your feet or that you pull out of the pile. Make up a story or an idea that explains why the three of them are connected. Now try it with the next three.

- *Memorize something.* Find some words you like: lyrics, sentences in a beautiful piece of prose, a classic poem, or speech from a movie. Memorize them. Even if it's just a minute or so of speech. If they're complicated, old words (Shakespeare or the Bible) say them out loud to yourself until they make sense. Look up the hard words. If it feels ridiculous, get a friend to join you. Once you've memorized them, congratulate yourself. The words are now yours. Not only can nobody take them away from you, but they are now somewhere deep inside your brain, imprinting their structure and beauty on whatever mysterious part of you knows how to make things. You'll find them cropping up in your own work in ways you could never have imagined.

- *Make a list.* Lists are a great way to procrastinate. But they can also be a great way to get your creative juices flowing. Make a list of: things that scare you, things that make you jealous, things that annoy you, things you regret, things you've forgotten, things you wish you could forget, people you wish you could meet, and so on. Nobody ever has to see your list.

- *Do your worst.* If you're a writer, draw. If you're a designer, write. If you make photos and movies, use words instead.

Try to get your message across in the way that makes you most uncomfortable. Don't worry about being any good. Just try to make others understand you.

- *Somebody else's problem.* Get out of your own head and go help somebody else. Your creative problem can wait. Go find somebody else with a project and offer to help. Get them to explain where they're stuck. Offer to do something to help, even if it's repetitive and mundane. Ask them to explain their project. You'll come back to your own project with a fresh set of eyes and at least one new idea to keep you moving.

- *Time travel.* If you're working on a problem that involves the Internet or another fairly recent technology, imagine that you've traveled back in time to ask for advice. You can talk to a famous person (Queen Victoria, Nikola Tesla, Elvis) or just somebody on the street. How do you explain your problem? Where do you start? What questions might they have? What assumptions are you making?

- *X marks the spot.* When we set out to do creative work, we're on a hunt for treasure. The solution, the finished article, the right image, the perfect pitch—none of them are inside us. We have to go in search of them. So make a map of your problem. Start with a big X. That's your destination. Now draw the pathway there, but be sure to put in all the obstacles on the way: the forest of vaguely defined goals, the desert of bad data, the river of distraction, the jungle of office politics, the maze of bureaucratic office procedures, the cave of possible failure. Is there a path around any of your obstacles? Were there obstacles you weren't aware of? Is there more than one X?

- *Amuse yourself.* You've heard of the Nine Muses—celestial ladies in flowing dresses who whispered lyrics into the ears of poets on mountaintops, waiting for inspiration to strike. But you don't have time to wait and you doubt a lady in a flowing dress is going to have much to say about the 400 words you need to write for the client by 5 P.M. Have no fear—the muse is still there. She (or he) just might look a little different in the twenty-first century. Write (or draw) a few lines, or find a photo online that represents who your muse is. Post it in view. When in need, ask for inspiration.

- *There's an app (or a bot) for that.* If artificial intelligence can beat the smartest humans at chess and Go, create convincing versions of Bach or Van Gogh, or pilot a car across hundreds of miles, then why hasn't somebody used it to solve your problem by now? What would a bot or an app need in order to do what you do? What would it need to do it better?

Connectivity

Aside from having distinct creativity, what separates successful content marketers and strategic communicators from those who are perceived as out of touch is an ability to truly connect with people.

Content created by other consumers, not brands, is 35 percent more memorable and 50 percent more trusted, according to research from the global research company Ipsos.[8] Why? Marketers aren't human enough. They aren't listening to consumers enough, engaging in meaningful conversations with them, or going off a corporate script to deliver better, bigger, more delightful customer experiences. And not enough brands are communicating values that individuals want to be affiliated with.

As I've said before, consumers today have many options, and more than ever they choose particular brands to communicate something personal about their own beliefs and priorities.[9] The best way to establish and reinforce common values is to create content that's so highly specific it defines not only the brand, but the customer.

Expressing a strong stance on social issues and taking action—to lessen the effects of climate change, source materials ethically, support hot-button legislation such as gay marriage, or donate a portion of profits to charity, for example—has become an expectation for consumers, especially millennials. According to a study by Horizon

---

[8]Max Knoblauch, "Millennials Trust User-Generated Content 50% More Than Other Media," Mashable, April 9, 2014, http://mashable.com/2014/04/09/millennials-user-generated-media/#z09BlD1EjGqY.

[9]Alexander Jutkowitz, "Marketing Is Dead, and Loyalty Killed It," *Harvard Business Review*, February 16, 2015, https://hbr.org/2015/02/marketing-is-dead-and-loyalty-killed-it?refresh.

Media, some 81 percent of millennials expect companies to make a public commitment to good corporate citizenship.[10] Another report by Mintel reveals that 56 percent of U.S. consumers will stop buying from companies they perceive are unethical.[11] At the time of this writing, in the early months of the Trump presidency, the pressure on brands to take sides on political issues has only increased. As one commentator put it, after the election of Trump, the "sidelines" disappeared from under our feet. It's no longer a differentiator for a brand to have some involvement in social issues; it's a requirement.

If you really want to connect with consumers, involve them as much as you can in your work.

Taylor Swift, arguably the music industry's best marketer, is the most adept at this. She has invited fans to her house to listen to her album before it drops as well as solicited their feedback on new material. Fans starred alongside her in the music video for "Shake It Off." And she pays extremely close attention to her supporters on social media—giving some Christmas presents as well as making her brokenhearted fans break-up playlists and giving them heartfelt advice. Her latest album *1989* included personal, hidden photos and messages to fans.[12] Collectively, these kinds of engagements led *1989* to sell a staggering 1.287 million copies in seven days, the single largest sales week for one album since 2002, when Eminem's *The Eminem Show* moved just over 1.3 million copies, according to *Forbes*.[13]

Of course, brands don't attract the same level of insane fandom as Swift does. But they can engage customers in smarter ways, such as

---

[10]Larissa Faw, "Millennials Expect More Than Good Products, Services to Win Their Loyalty," *Forbes*, May 22, 2014, www.forbes.com/sites/larissafaw/2014/05/22/millennials-expect-more-than-good-products-services-to-win-their-loyalty/#456fa2554d1c.

[11]Mintel, "56% of Americans Stop Buying from Brands They Believe Are Unethical," PR Newswire, November 18, 2015, www.prnewswire.com/news-releases/56-of-americans-stop-buying-from-brands-they-believe-are-unethical-300181141.html.

[12]Christina Garibaldi, "Here Are the Secret Messages Taylor Swift Hid on Her *1989* Album," MTV, September 27, 2014, www.mtv.com/news/1976527/taylor-swift-1989-hidden-messages/.

[13]Hugh McIntyre, "Taylor Swift's *1989* Moves 1.287 Million Copies in Its First Week," *Forbes*, November 5, 2014, www.forbes.com/sites/hughmcintyre/2014/11/05/taylor-swifts-1989-moves-1-287-million-copies-in-its-first-week/#6b46e71b3590.

leveraging user-generated content. Last summer Coca-Cola's "Share a Coke" campaign featured 250 popular names and colloquialisms such as "BFF" and "Bro" printed on labels where "Coca-Cola" would be printed and encouraged customers to share bottles with friends and family. Coca-Cola also asked consumers to share their experiences on Twitter with the hashtag #ShareaCoke and users who did had their photos featured on the company's website and on billboards. Coke saw a 2 percent jump in sales after introducing the campaign, and more than 500,000 photos were shared with the #ShareaCoke hashtag.[14] The brand also gained more than 25 million Facebook followers.

Millennials prefer people over brands, and 84 percent of the demographic say user-generated content (UGC) on company websites has at least some influence on what they buy, according to a Bazaarvoice report.[15] Additionally, 86 percent say that UGC is generally a good indicator of the quality of a brand or service. YouTube is a particularly powerful platform for UGC, with user-created video far outperforming brand-created videos. Of CoverGirl's 251 million total views, 99 percent are from fan-created videos,[16] and 99 percent of Revlon's views also come from fan content, according to *Forbes*.[17] Not only do fan-created makeup tutorials make these brands appear more authentic, it makes the process of content creation a heck of a lot easier to scale and it comes at a low cost. If you're concerned about the sheer hours it might take to comb through UGC, there are plenty of automation tools that surface quality content in real time.

Some brands have gone beyond promoting their own products, tying user-generated content to philanthropy to stand out in the realm of socially responsible businesses. Target asked customers to submit

---

[14]Ron Selvey, "Why Brands Should Embrace User-Generated Content," Experticity, June 23, 2015, https://business.experticity.com/why-brands-should-embrace-user-generated-content/.

[15]Bazaarvoice, "Talking to Strangers: Millennials Trust People over Brands," January 2012, http://media2.bazaarvoice.com/documents/Bazaarvoice_WP_Talking-to-Strangers.pdf.

[16]Zach James, "Fans Crush Brands When It Comes to YouTube," *Adweek*. June 13, 2013.

[17]"How Brands Can Make User-Generated Content Work for Them," *Forbes*, April 29, 2015, www.forbes.com/sites/onmarketing/2015/04/29/how-brands-can-make-user-generated-content-work-for-them/#44b164964f10.

videos of themselves opening college acceptance letters in 2010, and the best videos were featured in a company commercial, which highlighted a pledge to donate $1 billion to K–12 education causes.

And some marketers seem to have been inspired by the widely successful ALS challenge, which asked people to do something accessible, but odd enough to gain attention—pour a bucket of ice water over their heads or make a donation to the ALS Foundation for bragging rights that you did some good.

In the same vein is Chevrolet's "Purple Your Profile" campaign, in which users applied purple filters over their Facebook photos to raise cancer awareness and donations. The automaker raised more than $1 million for cancer organizations with that campaign and drove attention to its Road to Recovery program, which provides transportation to and from treatment for people who have cancer and do not have a ride.

Both campaigns relied on something easy to do, visible, and easy to share.

Ultimately, people want to be engaged in new ways and surprised. They want to feel special and valued, so get personal and really connect with fans individually. It makes lasting impact and in many cases delivers an immediate return on investment.

How Brands Evolve

Constant adaptation—refreshing old models as well as overhauling approaches entirely—is the necessary ingredient to relevancy in today's business world. Brands can't afford to stand still, even momentarily.

Typically, when successful companies fail, there are three reasons why, according to Vijay Govindarajan, a professor at Dartmouth's Tuck School of Business and coauthor of "The Other Side of Innovation."

1. They make big investments into old systems or equipment rather than new innovations.
2. Company leaders pride themselves on past success to the point that they ignore new competitors that threaten to outpace them.

3. They focus too heavily on the marketplace of today and fail to anticipate consumers' future needs.

Sometimes, companies' failures fall into all three categories—Blockbuster is a famous example. When Netflix founder Reed Hastings approached Blockbuster CEO John Antioco back in 2000 and proposed a partnership, he was laughed out of the room. Antioco later had multiple opportunities to buy Netflix for $50 million but never accepted. By the time Blockbuster launch its own DVD-by-mail business and rental kiosks, it couldn't compete with Netflix or Redbox. Failing to see how the home video industry was changing early on and overestimating his company's future success (Blockbuster was doing $6 billion in sales in 2004), Antioco inadvertently forced his company into bankruptcy by 2010.[18]

If brands don't evolve, they quickly become extinct, and the companies that have successfully evolved leverage ingenuity. Lego has proven its ability to constantly reinvent itself, through design-driven, highly covetable toys and branding across successful movies, product licensing deals with *Star Wars* and *Harry Potter*, international Legoland theme parks, and its innovations integrating technology with its hardware. An example of the latter—the popular Lego Fusion, which allows kids to build houses or castles with Legos, take photos of them, and watch the structures come to life in a virtual world in the Lego app. While Fusion sold well and was on the Toys"R"Us list of the 15 hottest Christmas toys, Fusion's creators told *Fast Company* that the product was, "at best a 1.0 version of a digital-physical play experience" that they were aiming to revolutionize.[19]

The basic Lego bricks haven't changed since 1963, but almost everything else about the company has, in part due to the genius of Lego's R&D team, Future Lab. Every global company has a research and development arm, but what makes this group different is its autonomy. Future Lab operates entirely separately from the rest of

[18]Thomas Gale, "Blockbuster Inc.," Encyclopedia.com www.encyclopedia.com/social-sciences-and-law/economics-business-and-labor/businesses-and-occupations/blockbuster-inc, accessed January 30, 2017.
[19]Jonathan Ringen, "How Lego Became the Apple of Toys," *Fast Company*, January 8, 2015, https://www.fastcompany.com/3040223/when-it-clicks-it-clicks.

the company's design groups, and only a handful of senior executives even have access to its building.

Most of what Future Lab builds doesn't see the light of day, but the learnings from its experiments have been momentous in helping the company innovate over the years. Lego CEO Jørgen Vig Knudstorp told *Fast Company*, "When you do such an exploration you become a lot more clever about everything from different business models to ways of developing a meaningful play experience. And you become wiser about the things you actually do launch."[20]

Over the years, Future Lab has partnered with MIT's Media Lab to build a robotics platform, launched an "open innovation platform" called Lego Ideas for fans to design and upload ideas to potentially be made into products, and hosted many 24-hour hackathons with industrial designers, interaction designers, programmers, ethnographic researchers, marketers, and master Lego builders to build better products. Now worth $7.1 billion and ranked number 86 on *Forbes'* most valuable brands list in 2016, the 84-year-old company cites its consumer-focused strategy as the secret to its success.

The most successful companies tend to loosen their grip on central control when it comes to fostering innovation as Lego does with its Future Lab.

I often hear CEOs say that "staying consistent" or "being timeless" is an ultimate goal for the brand. I tell them that being timeless isn't the same as avoiding change entirely. A brand can have a distinct personality, but it has to respond to the issues and concerns of the day for that personality to continue to express itself.

A company like General Electric hasn't survived since 1878 by staying rigidly the same. Rather, GE has evolved into many different markets over the last few decades, including health care, analytics and software, and energy. Innovations in each of these sectors are too numerous to name, but to highlight a few recent examples: a CT scanner that cuts radiation exposure in half, a hybrid locomotive that reduces emissions significantly, its brilliantly reengineered jet engine, and commercially viable OLED (organic light-emitting diode) lighting.

---

[20]Ibid.

Approach content the same way you'd approach exploring new markets to disrupt. Build a *culture* of creativity; allow for the open exchange of ideas as well as the flexibility for your team members to work independently, and involve your customers in your conversations as much as possible.

Insights

- Once the right people are on board with a shared vision, leadership should take a step back. Provide support when needed, but allow your creators to work independently. The personal touches of each individual are the mark of truly original content. It makes the brand one of a kind, which is what your customers want. Collectively, these personal touches are what set you apart from your competitors.
- Your people should come from all kinds of backgrounds. Attracting a diverse group of people with different backgrounds and ways of thinking should be a high priority.
- When it comes to inspiring creativity, everyone works differently, so allow your team to do what works best for it.
- To truly connect with your fans, involve them in your work, and have a conversation with them as much as possible.

Ask Yourself

- How can you recruit the right people to support your content efforts?
- Are you allowing your teams enough creative freedom? And are they creating their best work? How can you inspire them to be more creative?
- Are you interacting with your customers enough?

7

Content Marketing Applied Part 1

Content Marketing Applied: The Content Hub

SJR's idea to turn brands into their own publishers evolved during the financial crisis of 2007. Amid an economic collapse, everyone was nervous about the future, and there was constant discussion about how the United States would recover. Lawmakers were about to pump billions of taxpayer dollars into "shovel-ready projects" through the American Recovery and Reinvestment Act (widely known as "the Stimulus").

We were fascinated by it, and decided to create a blog that focused on infrastructure, energy, and sustainability—the areas that would create jobs and grow the economy. It featured news and thoughtful analysis written by journalists with true expertise in these areas. We called it *The Infrastructurist* and launched in 2009.

We had been market researchers and public relations specialists for master brands as well as strategists for politicians for many years, but our world was changing with the evolution of digital communication. For the sake of our longevity, our business had to expand its capabilities.

The Infrastructurist started as a passion project that filled a niche that other blogs in the world weren't filling at the time. And when we started it, we hadn't thought about how to monetize it. We just knew we had something interesting to say that people would want to read about.

As with many passion projects, we created something that the world ended up putting a very high value on. We created an engaged community with many subscribers who often discussed our work in the comments and on social media, and our blog was named a top blog in infrastructure. *The Infrastructurist* was ad free, and we never made a penny off it. If I could go back, I wouldn't change a thing.

It was *The Infrastructurist* that led me to the idea that brands could publish relevant industry news and analysis the same way a traditional publisher could. At the time, traditional media outlets were suffering; advertisers weren't biting for print, and publishers couldn't figure out how to properly monetize their digital operations, oscillating between whether to use paywalls or banner ads, which users hated. Unable to create a sustainable model, especially during a financial meltdown, publishers laid off hundreds of talented journalists and had to scale back significantly the quality work they were publishing.

There was a need to be filled, and an enormous business opportunity, wherein I realized that brands could tell relevant, engaging stories the same way *The Infrastructurist* had. In doing so, brands could get the exposure they always wanted from traditional media outlets but weren't able to land and then distribute it strategically. Ultimately brands could control the conversation, build stronger reputations, and possibly increase sales, if they said something people cared about.

As all of this was happening, we pitched a strategy for *GE Reports*, which we thought could be an online magazine about science, tech, and innovation on the same level as *Wired, Popular Science,* and *The Economist*'s science and technology section. Because of our proven success with *The Infrastructurist* and the detailed plan we developed for *GE Reports*, they gave us a shot, and *GE Reports* became SJR's first content marketing success—well before content marketing was part of the zeitgeist. We've told some incredible, exclusive stories with GE over the years, from scientific breakthroughs in health care to innovations in clean energy. We've helped GE manage its reputation as it has transformed itself from an industrial and consumer goods company to the world's pioneer of digital industrial technology.

It was the beginning of a new era in corporate communications; "middleweight content" was born.

The Process of Creating a Hub

Let's talk about what this means for you. How exactly do you build a content hub that fits seamlessly with the rest of your web properties, makes sense for your brand, and is highly engaging and different from what's already out there?

A thoughtful, high-level strategy from the outset is the first step to success. The more you can focus your message, the stronger your connection to your audience will be.

To truly become your own media company and create a community of engaged return visitors, earn media placements for your work, attract influential contributing guest bloggers, and gain a solid reputation in your field, you need to identify what truly makes your brand special and unearth industry knowledge as well as stories that people care about. Market research, comprehensive strategy, and careful planning (long-term and short-term) will help get you there.

Here's what that process looks like. Then we'll get into how to approach each element of your hub.

THE BASICS OF CREATING A CONTENT HUB, AND WHAT TO CONSIDER FOR EACH STAGE

Stage 1: Early Goals

- Conduct high-level market research. Understand how your target audiences consume information and what topics matter to them.
- Who are your competitors and what are they saying? Understand other publishers and where you can stand out.
- Develop a clear approach to what content to publish, when, and where.
- Determine how to measure and adapt based on how the content performs.
- Build your team. Who will be the managing editor of the hub? Who will write, design, produce multimedia, do social, and help with ongoing strategy within your organization?
- Get buy in from key stakeholders and align on concept for the hub. Determine the budget for the project.

Stage 2: Discovery

- Dig into who you're trying to reach. Beyond traditional demographics, who is your audience? What is their mind-set? What can you own in the content space, and how can we give them a unique experience?
- Your review of industry conversations should span both traditional competitors, other content competitors that are writing about related topics, traditional publishers, along with best in class content publishers. It includes research on search trends, social conversations, SEO landscape via tagging analysis, and competing content through other owned media properties.
- Know what your potential audience is searching for and conduct contextual search analysis in areas of relevant interest

and develop content strategies that answer the questions your
audience is seeking in its search behaviors. This is broader than
keyword strategy; a smart content strategy focuses more on
natural language processing of key phrases and queries that
trend high on search indices.

- Research which platforms and content formats are best to reach
  your audience. Decide on an ideal publishing cadence (which
  you can adapt as you produce content and measure
  performance).

- Determine what counts as a conversion—what action do you
  want your users to take after they've visited your hub? Set key
  performance indicators and be willing to revise them as
  necessary.

Stage 3: Editorial Strategy

- Craft a mission statement and guidelines around tone and
  voice, identify pillars for the website and the points you're
  bringing to the conversation, decide how you'll gather
  interesting visuals for the site, and determine what your brand
  doesn't want to be or get involved in.

- Determine logistics for content creation and approval. How
  will your team work together, and how will these individuals
  work together to ideate and unearth organizational
  knowledge? Will any content need legal review?

- Strategize social and paid distribution.

- Educate the team on best SEO practices and align on goals and
  style/tone for the website.

**Stage 4: Build Your Website, Design an Exemplary
User Experience**

- As you prepare your website for launch, strategize how to
  create a seamless user experience. How can the stories best
  be told in an engaging, digestible way? What is the right format
  based on the channels you're using? What type of content do
  audiences best digest? How can you establish a consistent
  visual identity? And consider how you'll personalize it.

- Design for mobile. Create a responsive web style to ensure that you're delivering an engaging user experience (UX) regardless of screen size and platform. Go mobile first without compromising the integrity of the features. Simplify the UX design with a primary navigation.

- Think through every bell and whistle, every plug-in to determine its effectiveness and necessity. Less is often more.

- Test your website as much as possible before launching, and have plenty of content for each pillar, ideally in multiple formats, ready for the launch.

Stage 5: Launch and Beyond

- Develop a thoughtfully planned editorial calendar and conduct regular team meetings for ideation, status of content, and any issues that might arise.

- Conduct ongoing strategy sessions and constantly measure traffic, users' reactions to content, and overall effectiveness. Constantly iterate based upon findings.

- Explore partnerships with different agencies, influencers, and freelancers to bring creativity and new talent on board.

- Work to create a sustaining creative culture of content marketing, where many teams across the company, business partners, and outside organizational connections are contributing to the storytelling and helping identify interesting stories.

Thought Leadership

A great brand is a mixture of many things. It is products, services, and places bearing a particular name and logo that exist as tangible, useful things in people's lives. It's also a set of perceptions and associations in the mind of the public. And it's also a set of people working for the brand at any given time.

Thought leadership is almost entirely concerned with that last attribute of a brand, the people. So many companies are willing to put their products into the world but are unwilling to let the people who believe in them the most—the people who make those products or design those services—speak on their behalf.

This is the primary function of thought leadership, which is the current phrase attached to a bundle of services meant for the leadership: speech writing, event and social content support, and personal brand development. Think of it as executive communications expanded and accelerated for the digital media landscape.

When providing thought leadership to top executives at some of the world's largest and most famous brands, I've noticed a curious phenomenon. Take a woman or a man who has the confidence and skill to lead tens of thousands of employees in multibillion dollar businesses and ask them to express a point of view to the public, even on a narrowly defined area of their expertise, and they freeze. Their sense of their own qualifications suddenly vanishes.

This is where it's helpful to remember how the advent of digital communications and social media is transforming the world we live in. And that executive communications, like any content from a company, can be transformative.

With social media in 2017, we are where TV was in the 1940s—at the birth of a new form of communication. We don't all have to be present on every new platform, but everyone is expected to have some niche in our shared digital common space, where people can go to get a sense of who they are and what they stand for. This is especially true of people in leadership roles.

In the absence of such a niche, people will begin to construct one for you, and fill it with their own version of your and your brand's identity.

Both for the strength of your brand's public image and as a way to build a stronger connection between your company's employees and its leaders, it's essential to build thought leadership into your overall digital strategy.

Your leaders should be communicating with strategic intention. Thought leadership content shouldn't be all about the brand, but it should reflect the leader's knowledge, interest, and perspective.

The goal is to elevate the writer and ultimately the company, organically. At every turn, the executive should be educating, inspiring, or entertaining the reader in no matter how small a way.

When done well, thought leadership makes writers more human and adds to their credibility.

Approach every piece of thought leadership content by asking these three questions: "Is this worth saying right now? Should the client be the one to say it? Will people be interested?" Narrow the gap between how people perceive you and how you want to be perceived with valuable thought leadership work, and make sure that it makes sense coming from you at that particular moment.

Bill Gates didn't wake up one day and decide to start writing about malaria. He made it his mission to eradicate the disease, as well as many others, and started talking about it after he had established that it was a defining personal ambition. As you begin to think about your personal reputation and your long-term goals, you have to think about how each piece of content ladders up to a greater mission, otherwise your words, no matter how well spoken, will hang in a vacuum.

Careful strategy should also be balanced with timely reactions to what your customers care about and what's happening in the world. If the Supreme Court is voting on same-sex marriage, and your company has been a big proponent of such legislation over the years, speak your mind with confidence. If there's an environmental issue and you work for a retailer like Levi Strauss and Company, with a reputation for innovating sustainable practices and minimizing environmental impact, move quickly to get your point across.

My other piece of advice is to build in some expectation of unpredictability in the public's response to your message. Not everyone will be your biggest fan, and that's perfectly fine. There's no way of knowing how your work will resonate without putting it out into the universe. And for those in heavily regulated industries, even a mild perspective will humanize you and help make you relevant.

Avoid what in SJR parlance is called "thought manufacturing." This is a situation where the strategic need for a leader to communicate and that leader's willingness to express anything related to his actual perspective doesn't overlap at all. This leaves the thought leadership team grasping at straws about what to say, often under considerable time pressure, and much of their work, however high in quality, is bound to miss the mark.

In cases such as these, it's best to engage not the leader herself but a trusted adviser who is willing to advance the work—and make quick executive judgments about what can be said and what will be approved. This will ensure that there is consistency to the work, without which good thought leadership cannot thrive.

There will often be situations in which a leader has to speak such as when the company has been publicly attacked or praised or when global affairs demand a response. These crisis situations, far from being moments of vulnerability, are the moments when the thought leadership team can prove its worth and gain more direct access to the leader its members serve. It requires all the nerve and skill of any firm that specializes in crisis communications, but it is well worth the effort. When the thought leadership team and the executive client learn to speak with one voice in a moment of crisis, the cohesive effect can be lasting, and powerful, and valuable to a company's reputation.

Have a Strong Visual Vocabulary

DESIGN

It's been said that we're in a golden age of design where clean aesthetics and functionality are deeply considered at every stage of the user experience. Creating an experience as Steve Jobs did with the iPhone, which is simply beautiful and so meticulously designed that anyone can use it, has become the core mission for virtually every tech entrepreneur and product designer.

While it's refreshing that design is being given its fair due and seen as more than colors, typography, layout and graphics, this awakening has been a long time coming.

The best design is human-centered. It transfers knowledge by default. There are plenty of examples over the course of history.

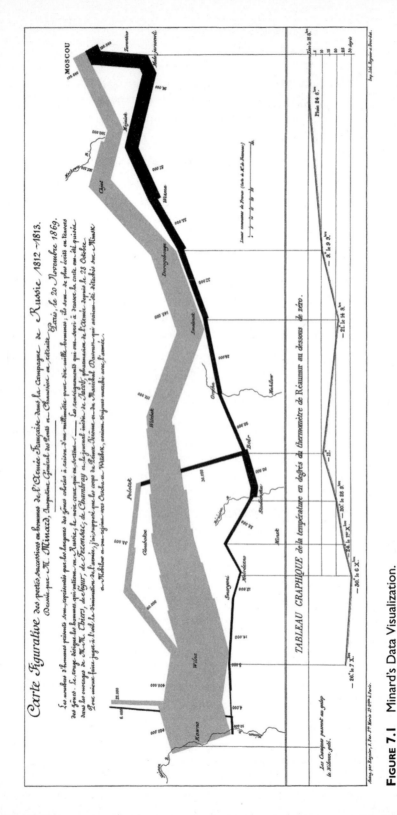

FIGURE 7.1 Minard's Data Visualization.

Source: https://en.wikipedia.org/wiki/Charles_Joseph_Minard

In 1812, a French engineer named Charles Joseph Minard created what is widely considered to be the best data visualization (see Figure 7.1). Balancing detail with clarity, he mapped Napoleon's troops march through Russia.[1] He included loss of life, time and location, temperature, geography, and historical context all in one graphic, without distracting text or labels. Information-rich without being overly cluttered or hard to read, the visualization was recognized as great by a number of cartographers. Famed French scientist, physiologist, and chronophotographer Étienne-Jules Marey said it "defies the pen of the historian in its brutal eloquence."[2]

A more recent example of brilliant design: Michael Bierut's New York City street and subway maps that keep millions of New Yorkers from getting lost.[3]

When asked how he stays creative, Bierut told *Wired* that he "doesn't believe in creativity"—at least not for creativity's sake—it has to be used deliberately within the parameters of clarity, intuition, and logic.[4]

This is how we should all be thinking about design. It's arguably the most important part of a content hub, as crucial as the quality of the content itself. We need to implement design thinking at every stage of production.

So how exactly does one do that?

Ask Questions and Then Problem Solve. To be most effective, designers need to be asking a lot of questions, and they really need

---

[1]Michael Sandberg, "DataViz History: Charles Minard's Flow Map of Napolean's Russian Campaign of 1812," Data Visualization blog, May 26, 2013, https://datavizblog.com/2013/05/26/dataviz-history-charles-minards-flow-map-of-napoleons-russian-campaign-of-1812-part-5/.

[2]Michael Sandberg, "DataViz History: Edward Tufte, Charles Minard, Napoleon and the Russian Campaign of 1812—Part 2," May 18, 2013, https://datavizblog.com/2013/05/18/dataviz-history-edward-tufte-charles-minard-napoleon-and-the-russian-campaign-of-1812-part-2/.

[3]Liz Stinson, "NYC'S Awesome New Map System Won't Leave You Lost," *Wired*, July 1, 2013, https://www.wired.com/2013/07/nyc-signs/.

[4]Liz Stinson, "Famed Designer Michael Bierut Doesn't Believe in Creativity," *Wired*, September 15, 2015, https://www.wired.com/2015/10/famed-designer-michael-bierut-doesnt-believe-in-creativity/.

to be focused on finding answers through A/B testing and talking to users. "How do we get our audience to click through our photo galleries?" "How do we get our users to discover content that they're most interested in within a few seconds of finishing an article?" "How do we balance keeping our page fresh with new material while maintaining the option of featuring certain pieces prominently?" From the get-go, these are the kinds of questions designers should be asking. They shouldn't be afraid to question what they've created, either.

Above All Else, Tell a Story. Designers need to create a visual vocabulary in their work to weave a narrative with a beginning, middle, and end through simple, intuitive interactions. The story should come before the visual execution, and designers should resist the temptation to build for a platform or a visual gimmick. With each design, it's important to ask, what are you really trying to say? And, most important, why should the user care?

Routinely Gather User Feedback and Iterate. Make time to talk to people—formally with A/B tests and informally through short in-person conversations. Even if you don't have a full design ready, talk through your rough prototypes and ideas to uncover opportunities for improvement. Be a constant learner who's totally open to discovering ways to make the experience better and more valuable. Follow Lean Startup founder Eric Ries' minimum viable product model, in which you show products that contain just the basic features sufficient to be functional in order to test your hypothesis without investing too much time engineering—this is how you remain agile and accelerate learning.

Allow Users to Discover and Design Features That Make It Easier to Stay Engaged. How will you keep users on your website? Related content selections placed above the fold can funnel users deeper into the site, and recommendations strategically located above the footer will capture and reengage those who scroll all the way to the bottom of the page. Personalization tools that help you get to know your users through data stored in cookies or through users' log-in information, can help serve relevant content. But it's also about the fine details, such as your verbiage for "related content," the thumbnails accompanying articles, and the physical layout that can make a user want to stick around.

Make It a Team Effort. Can't stress this enough. As I said in the last chapter, the most successful designers don't operate in a vacuum. They work alongside a fully inclusive team in which each member is free to express his unique perspective. Ownership of projects should be shared—this keeps everyone engaged and motivated to do their best work.

The Sensory Experience. Brands can't define themselves by words alone; images, video, interactives, GIFs, podcasts, infographics, and immersive experiences all tell stories of their own.

We're visual learners and thinkers. When people hear information, they're likely to remember only 10 percent of that information three days later.[5] However, if a relevant image is paired with that same information, people retain 65 percent of it three days later. This holds true for a compelling image with an interesting photo caption, as *National Geographic* demonstrates on its Instagram channel, as well as a clean and straightforward data visualization, which the *New York Times* does exceptionally well.

In a world where content is spread across multiple platforms and the platforms are increasingly idiosyncratic—GIFs are better suited for Tumblr's audience over Pinterest's, for example—we need to carefully consider whether we're speaking the same language that each audience does. You can take one single message and splice it several ways to craft a unique angle for different mediums and platforms. And like the podcast *Serial* or Netflix's *Making a Murderer*, you should be thinking about ways to divide your most compelling stories into episodes to keep your audience engaged.

The hardest part is figuring out what your story is and how it's different from what's already out there. From there, you can engage all five of your audience's senses and atomize your message for

---

[5]John Medina, "Brain Rules," Pear Press, www.brainrules.net/vision, accessed January 31, 2017.

different platforms to create a digital ecosystem full of complexity and personal interaction.

Two issues of SJR's quarterly digital magazine, *Unfiltered*, sought to demonstrate these concepts: atomization, splicing one message over different mediums and platforms, and serialization, telling one story over multiple episodes. (For more on these concepts, see Chapter 5.)

The atomization issue explored the topic scent, and our team created GIFs of a woman smelling a scent, a business story about the state of the perfume industry, a podcast with a neuroscience researcher at the University of California, San Diego who is unable to smell, an illustrated map and photo essay of scents across Manhattan, and a short man-on-the-street-style video (as well as a Snapchat story) of people answering, "What does New York City smell like?" I also wrote about how marketers can tell stories with scent.

For the serialization issue, we stuck to written stories with a highly compelling set of images. We did a story about our favorite serialized true crime shows, from HBO's *The Wire* to Netflix's *Orange Is the New Black*; a story about how serialized storytelling has been creating community since 1933, with President Franklin Delano Roosevelt's fireside chats; a listicle about how brands can execute serialization without falling flat; and I wrote about rich and deep communication in an age of serialized storytelling.

For these issues, and for every issue, there's a lot of strategy and planning up front. Our team of writers, artists, photographers, and designers evaluates and reevaluates how each piece fits into the greater whole, tweaking concepts along the way, and meeting several times to brainstorm execution and logistics. In an ideal world, this is how brands should operate when they tell stories.

VIDEO

To be most effective, all multimedia has to be optimized for mobile on your hub—70 percent of Internet use is now on a mobile device, and the use of desktop machines for Internet access will fall by almost 16 percent by the end of 2016, according to Zenith's Media

Consumption Forecasts.[6] It's critical that your team is thinking about the mobile experience from the ideation stage. Of all media formats, mobile optimization is especially important for video.

Currently, every social media company is focused on optimizing its platforms for video, with usage soaring. The number of average daily video views on Facebook doubled from 4 billion views per day to 8 billion between April 2015 and November 2015 alone. Facebook is testing a dedicated video feed where people can browse different channels of videos shared by friends, trending on Facebook, and other themes, according to *TechCrunch*. It's also testing how it can get users to watch videos as they scroll through their feeds, by optimizing them to run as a thumbnail in the right-hand corner of the screen as you browse. The company is also considering a prominently positioned option to save a video to watch later.[7]

But we can't treat video like a 30-second TV spot; if you're overtly trying to sell something, you'll quickly lose your audience. The Internet has subtly but fundamentally different rules from broadcast television.

One of my favorite examples of branded entertainment is *Breakthrough*, a documentary series by National Geographic and GE on cutting-edge scientific innovations. The series focused on scientific discoveries, with one episode diving into global pandemics such as Ebola, HIV, influenza, malaria, and other diseases and exploring innovations in neuroscience, anti-aging technology, alternative energy, and water conservation. Ron Howard and Brian Grazer produced the series, and Paul Giamatti, Brett Ratner, Akiva Goldsman, Peter Berg, and Angela Bassett, as well as Howard directed the episodes.

The series was a gripping, in-depth look at complex topics with insights about how far science has come and an outline for the

---

[6]Jemma Brackebush, "How Mobile Is Overtaking Desktop for Global Media Consumption, in 5 Charts," *Digiday*. June 14, 2016, http://digiday.com/publishers/mobile-overtaking-desktops-around-world-5-charts/.

[7]Johs Constine, "Facebook Hits 8 Billion Daily Video Views, Doubling from 4 Billion in April," *TechCrunch*, November 4, 2015, https://techcrunch.com/2015/11/04/facebook-video-views/.

future. It evenhandedly presented the challenges as well as promise of today's research. In terms of how it was branded, GE helped pick the topics for the series and gave the producers access to its research centers to generate story ideas, and there were some interviews with GE scientists throughout. GE took a hands-off approach to the production.

The sole mission of the series was to enlighten, interest, and entertain the viewer. At the end of the day, the goal was to make you think and feel and encourage you to learn more about the world.

Whether you're shooting a docuseries or a branded series of 10-second clips for a social platform, always make sure your message has value—that you're educating or demonstrating how to do something, taking your audience to an event, entertaining them, or interacting with them.

Live video has become vastly popular across Facebook, Twitter, Instagram, Snapchat, and Periscope, giving users unfettered, often unscripted behind-the-scenes access that people crave from the accounts they follow. Don't be afraid to go off script and allow your brand's personalities to improvise on the spot with live and regular videos.

Fashion designers, including Tommy Hilfiger, Jeremy Scott, and Carolina Herrera used Periscope to live stream their Fashion Week shows, with the platform becoming the industry's most popular direct-to-consumer channel, and some brands using it to inform business decisions when users comment on the stream about what they think of the clothing.

On Facebook Live, more than 665,000 people tuned in to Adidas Women's channel on International Yoga Day when it featured two 45-minute yoga sessions with famed yoga and fitness influencer Adriene Mishler. Mishler wore Adidas clothing, which I bet sold a lot right after the live stream, and the stream showcased Adidas' commitment to its customers' healthy lifestyles, which carries a long-term value.

Question and answer live streams with experts also make brands feel more connected. NASA collaborated with the Smithsonian in October 2016 so experts could discuss and answer questions about topics related to NASA's journey to Mars and other missions. And Benefit Cosmetics partnered with *Glamour* U.K. to give viewers the opportunity to ask all kinds of beauty questions, and the hosts did live demonstrations. Those are two example of true two-way communication, the kind with the potential to turn your fans into loyalists and make them feel heard.

IMAGES, ILLUSTRATIONS, INFOGRAPHICS, AND INTERACTIVES

Your brand is competing with millions of photos, videos, interactives, GIFs, and infographics each day on the Internet, and we're bombarded by way more information on the Internet than our brains are able to fully process and remember. We spend an average of 8 hours and 10 minutes consuming some sort of media each day, and by 2017, we'll be closer to 8.5 hours, according to research. Most of that media consumption is on the Internet, particularly on our smartphones.[8]

In the past, media consumption was a much more passive experience—we'd watch television or listen to the radio. With the rise of digital platforms and smartphones, our media consumption has become increasingly interactive, with frequently interrupted viewership and multitasking happening, while we watch.

This means that your brand has a very small window of opportunity to stand out. So your creative has to be even more relevant, eye-catching, and meaningful to the audience, otherwise it will be drowned out in the noise.

There are some visuals on the Internet that just stick with us. They transcend language and cultural barriers, and traditional concepts of literacy to connect with audiences on an emotional level.

I'm not talking about stock photos—unless we're talking about the hilariously staged stock photos that everyone loves to hate, regardless of your age, race, gender, and socioeconomic status. I'm not talking about the stereotypical images that come from a corporate visual assets library, such as highly edited product shots, nor your brand's spin on the latest viral meme.

---

[8]Jason Karaian, "We Now Spend More than Eight Hours a Day Consuming Media," *Quartz*, November 4, 2015, https://techcrunch.com/2015/11/04/facebook-video-views/.

I'm talking about *compelling*, original images.

Some of the images in each of our *Unfiltered* issues are unlike anything I've ever seen. For the serialization issue, our creative director went for a retro, vintage look that drew inspiration from catalogs and magazine ads from the late 1960s or early 1970s (see Figure 7.2).

Like compelling images, infographics and interactives need to *say something*. They need to be totally original and different from what's already on the Internet in order for it to be worth the time, effort, and cost to produce them.

Some people think infographics are overhyped, but when done right, infographics make complex information easy to comprehend.

FIGURE 7.2   Unfiltered One.

Source: Unfiltered, "Serialization," Group SJR, http://unfiltered.groupsjr.com/serialization/, accessed January 30, 2017.

They make raw data, dense reports, and white papers digestible, democratizing information for users. And when they tell a compelling story, infographics and interactives are very sticky, meaning they stick in users' minds and show up on their social feeds. Infographics are liked and shared on social media three times more than any other type of content.[9]

According to research from Hubspot, 90 percent of the information passed to the brain is visual, which the brain processes faster and more easily.[10] Therefore, it's unsurprising that 40 percent of people respond better to visual information compared to plain text.

Great infographics and interactives tell a story; they have a beginning, middle, and end. They are equal parts art and science—with function and the user experience more important than overindulgent fashion. Designers need to be careful not to unwittingly distort the data to fit a decorative scheme. They must be created with precision, care, and integrity.

As infographics become more ubiquitous, users are becoming more literate in reading charts, diagrams, and graphic representations of data.[11] As a result, producers of infographics—from marketers to brands and designers—will need to be more mindful in what they create.

My best advice is don't create an infographic or an interactive for the sake of creating it. I can't emphasize that enough; you need to have a compelling reason to tell a story in pictures. And any added animations need to advance the story you're telling. Every digital element needs to serve a purpose, just as Minard illustrated back in 1812 with his map.

---

[9]Johnny, "10 Types of Visual Content to Use in Your Content Marketing," Mass Planner, October 21, 2015, www.massplanner.com/10-types-of-visual-content-to-use-in-your-content-marketing/.

[10]Amanda Sibley, "19 Reasons You Should Include Visual Content in Your Marketing [Image]," HubSpot, August 6, 2012, https://blog.hubspot.com/blog/tabid/6307/bid/33423/19-Reasons-You-Should-Include-Visual-Content-in-Your-Marketing-Data.aspx#sm.00001ryhldmh8bdm5vmcjjnea4mit.

[11]*Unfiltered*, "Show, Not Tell: The Immortal Infographic," Group SJR, http://unfiltered.groupsjr.com/show-not-tell-the-immortal-infographic/, accessed January 30, 2017.

Emerging Platforms

Our technology is steadily become more relatable, more human. Natural language processing systems, such as Siri and Google Now, are getting better at understanding us. Cognitive computing systems can predict our needs before we consciously think of them. Wearables can track our biological functions with great precision—there are even mood-sensing technologies and high-tech headbands such as Muse that can help us meditate. Technology is becoming an ever more seamless extension of ourselves, and in the future it will be integrated into our day-to-day lives as pervasively and invisibly as earlier technologies, like clocks and electricity.

While that is unsettling to some people, I see it as an opportunity. We're at the outer edge of a digital revolution akin to the beginning of the Industrial Revolution in the mid-1700s.

As marketers and strategic communicators, experimentation with new technologies should be constant, and we shouldn't be afraid of failing in the course of discovery. By the time you read this book, I'm certain there will have been dozens of examples of brands exploring new storytelling frontiers. I hope yours is one of them.

So here's my permission to dabble in virtual reality, augmented reality, and mixed reality. Go ahead and create 4-D experiences. Build interactive, shoppable windows in areas with high foot traffic. Consider integrating unique scent and touch into your story to make in-person experiences sensory. Venture into lesser-known territory to create unexpected experiences for your fans. Figure out how to express your brand's core personality in a new way and make your mark. For the nervous entrant, as long as you stay true to your identity and put the user at the center of the experience, your experiment is going to be okay! And even interesting failures are bound to get your brand attention.

The Best Content Hubs...

Have one primary navigation. While there's no one right way to design a website's navigation, it should be as simple as possible, with few tabs and no drop-down menus.

Overwhelming your user with choices and using too much text will hamper the experience. Package your website so content is discoverable in a way that doesn't make the user have to click too many times to get to a new piece of content. When site structure is optimized for content discoverability, you'll likely find the number of navigation options going down.

Integrate microsites. Don't create dead ends. Your hub doesn't exist in a bubble. Include a clear way to navigate to other owned properties from the microsite to lower bounce rates and increase conversions (if that's the goal). Search engines will reward you for this.

Highlight new content. Switch your featured content often—at least once a day—so that visitors keep coming back. For any digital content feed, from a twitter account to the front page of a newspaper, a once-daily refresh of content is optimal.

Label content clearly and descriptively. Generic pillar labels like "News" don't communicate what the user will find when they navigate there. Save visitors the click (and help reduce your bounce rate) by making your website navigation descriptive.

Have fully functional search. Make your search bar prominent on the homepage, and ensure it's wide enough for long strings of text. Your search functionality has to be smart, and you can improve it by mining your web analytics data to determine what users are actually searching and adjusting accordingly. Implement a natural language processing-enabled search engine rather than a basic keyword engine so users are able to search fluidly, with terms that make intuitive sense. Adjust search for mobile as well, with features such as autocomplete to account for misspellings on smaller screens. Lastly, give users the ability to refine queries by using variables like type, topic, author, date, and geography.

Make SEO standard. More important than putting spend behind your hub is making it sticky enough that users can find it organically. Being consistent is key, which means it's imperative that everyone involved with the hub—from writers and designers to the social team—is properly educated on best practices. Make sure everyone is tagging images, adding inbound and outbound links, filling out the metadata, and using keywords on each page. An HTML and

XML sitemap needs to be created from the start. These are a few foundational best practices, but I'd advise consulting an SEO expert who can give ongoing advice most pertinent to your website.

Consider the full distribution ecosystem. Social media should never be an afterthought. From the outset, plan content creation around how it will be tailored to each platform and test your atomized pieces in creative ways across your accounts. Secondly, develop partnerships with influencers and media outlets for syndication of content, and proactively engage both as content is being developed with the goal of driving awareness and amplifying content. Also invite influencers to create content for your site and cross promote it through your social channels and theirs. And, of course, consider paid media against search, social, and sponsored content—paid is especially important in the early stages of a website launch to drive awareness.

Measure and pivot. The ability to leverage analytics will be crucial to your hub's success. Measure, learn, and iterate. Use a platform like Single Score, which is a customizable algorithm to measure ROI and define success. The dashboard should be tailored to the company's strategy and digital footprint, offering a daily, comprehensive overview of earned, owned, paid, and competitive benchmarking in one place.

Internal Communications

Most strategic communicators treat internal corporate communications as an afterthought, which is an enormous lost opportunity. The days of the corporate newsletter are long over, as are the days when that was enough to capture the attention of your employees. Most executives recognize the need to keep people informed about the company's strategy and direction, but few understand the need to *excite* employees about the brand's power and tell its best stories. Also, many times internal communications falls on the shoulders of HR professionals, who may lack the communications skills to take full advantage of the opportunity.

Internal communications can do everything content marketing can do for a brand. At best, internal communications has the potential to transform how a company operates.

But what better way to raise corporate reputation than with a company's most important asset: the employees themselves? If we put as much effort into internal communications as we did external communications, employees would have a stronger emotional connection to their work that would make them more motivated, and they'd feel more loyalty toward the company—a necessary aspiration for companies in today's business landscape, with only 32 percent of employees engaged in their work.[12] Employees would also have more knowledge about what's going on in the industry and the company's place in it, and feel more unified by a common sense of purpose and identity. In the process, a strong communications program would trigger different departments to share their knowledge and customer stories with the communications team, which would make for better storytelling across the board.

Exceptional internal communications can have real implications for company profits. In 1992, Arthur Martinez was named head of Sears' merchandising group during a time when sales were in the gutter. On sales of $52.3 billion, the company's net loss was $3.9 billion, almost $3 billion of which came from the merchandising group, according to *Harvard Business Review* (HBR).[13] It was a culmination of negative factors, but most of them attributed to the company's lack of focus. Martinez made it his mission to energize and focus employees. He created task forces of senior managers, which spent months listening to customers and employees, studying best practices at other companies, thinking about what would constitute world-class performance at Sears, and establishing measures and objectives. The task forces surveyed workers, held focus groups and

---

[12]Amy Adkins, "Employee Engagement in U.S. Stagnant in 2015," Gallup, January 13, 2016, www.gallup.com/poll/188144/employee-engagement-stagnant-2015.aspx.
[13]Anthony J. Rucci, Steven P. Kirn, and Richard T. Quinn, "The Employee-Customer-Profit Chain at Sears," *Harvard Business Review*, January–February 1998, https://hbr.org/1998/01/the-employee-customer-profit-chain-at-sears.

town hall meetings, and honed in on personal development to build a workforce of high-growth involved and empowered employees. The results of the efforts were stunning, with the multibillion-dollar loss turning into a $725 million profit in the first year alone and a total shareholder return of 56 percent, according to HBR.[14]

Needless to say, this is an extreme example of the positive results of effective internal communications, but it's proof of how robust an opportunity it is.

Ultimately, there should be no sharp difference between internal and external communications—both should convey one cohesive identity and message and leverage different mediums to tell stories. Videos, interactives, podcasts, and so forth can be created for employees to build that emotional connection with the company and the brand.

Turn your year-end financial report into an easy-to-comprehend data visualization for employees, for example. Use customized channels for specific announcements through platforms such as Slack. Take boring training manuals and turn them into short, creative, even funny how-to videos. Build a knowledge-sharing platform that will enable employees to teach each other new skills and make stronger personal connections in the process.

In addition, you can build a unified communications strategy with a centralized internal and external hub. For example, Target's A Bullseye View has lifestyle, online magazine-style stories, such as exclusive interviews with Taylor Swift under its News and Features tab, but the navigation also leads to the corporate site, which includes Target's purpose and beliefs, history, stock information, and annual reports. While this works for Target, it might not be possible for every company. But a unified website is certainly worth exploring, as the goal should always be to align external and internal perceptions of the company's integrity and mission.

---

[14]Andrea Ovans, "Sears Has Come Back from the Brink Before," *Harvard Business Review*, October 28, 2014, https://hbr.org/2014/10/sears-has-come-back-from-the-brink-before.

Regardless of how internal communications looks in practice, try to keep it free of corporate speak. Your employees can be your best storytellers and a major source of marketing inspiration. When Miller Brewing Company conducted an in-depth study aimed at measuring employee attitudes for the sake of improving morale, company leaders learned that employees took great pride in the company's tradition of brewing, mythologized by stories such as that of founder Frederick Miller carrying the yeast in his pocket from Germany in 1855.[15] The internal campaign leveraged those messages and became a celebration of employees' passion for great beer. The company hung large posters of employees in the breweries, depicting workers as company heroes and distributed materials reinforcing the campaign, including a book celebrating the vocation of brewing and T-shirts emblazoned with "I Make Miller Time." The brand's heritage of craftsmanship, which came from employees' perception, became a focal point of consumer advertising, with new TV commercials featuring employees talking to the camera and expressing their passion for Miller beer. And as HBR points out, the focus on internal research by collecting stories like that of Frederick Miller ensures that company folklore doesn't walk out the door when veteran employees leave, which preserves the culture for future generations of employees. If communication becomes a truly democratic, collaborative effort, where employees outside of the communications team tell their stories and impart their wisdom, the result is powerful.

For internal e-mails from executives, ask yourself why can't one-way communications be two-way? How about instead of that lifeless e-mail, the CEO holds an in-person fireside chat or Google Hangout for remote employees, and gives them the opportunity to ask anything? Treat your employees better than you would your customers, and listen to them more than you speak. An open door policy will work wonders for your business.

---

[15]Colin Mitchell, "Selling the Brand Inside," *Harvard Business Review*, January 2002, https://hbr.org/2002/01/selling-the-brand-inside.

Insights

- Developing a strong strategy before you build a website is absolutely critical, because it has to fit well with the rest of your web properties, make sense for your brand, and be highly engaging and different from what's already out there.

- No matter what format your content takes, whether it's thought leadership bylines, video, interactive infographics, GIFs, or written stories, make sure you're *saying something*—something that uniquely entertains, inspires, and educates. And make sure that it aligns with your business goals. Remember, every piece of content you create fits into a larger image that your brand is building. Don't forget your purpose and values or why you started. At the same time, don't get hung up if every single piece of content doesn't resonate with your audience. It's a learning experience, for better or for worse.

- Internal communications matter just as much as external communications. Take each communication as an opportunity to share your brand's best stories or to create platforms for people to exchange their own stories.

Ask Yourself

- How will I go about finding stories that people actually care about and unearth my company history? How will I get other units and people within the company comfortable sharing stories, some of which might be more about the industry as a whole and less about my company's offerings?

- Who is best suited to author thought leadership pieces? Who are the experts and people with interesting stories to tell? Keep in mind that it's okay to think beyond the C-suite.

- How can I ensure my hub is as user-friendly as possible?

- How can I create more unique sensory experiences for people to experience my brand? Or leverage emerging platforms to tell better stories?

- How can we improve our internal communications strategy to tell engaging stories?

8

Content Marketing Applied Part 2

Knowledge Transfer: Putting It All Together

When brands have all the pieces in place, and they're publishing compelling content each day as a traditional publisher would, their work becomes bigger than the brand itself. They're no longer just marketing to consumers or other businesses. They're transferring knowledge that teaches, entertains, and inspires people. The most valuable work will stick with people.

When your work is meaningful, people don't just sit up and take notice. *They don't forget it.*

Strive to make an indelible impression on your audience, and think far beyond your products and services and the confines of your company's walls. Think about what *matters* to people and deliver the high-value creative work that they won't be able to forget. It's the only way to truly move the needle for your brand and improve lives—because it's not a stretch to say that truly meaningful knowledge can improve people's lives. After all, journalists improve our lives, and talented content marketers aren't that much different.

Transferring knowledge requires fluency across multiple platforms and a distinctly strategic approach to each. When companies are overreliant on the separate units that comprise them, it can hamper this fluency. Content marketing teams aren't always looped into the social or advertising teams' plans, for example, and different lines of business aren't aware of each other's initiatives or focuses of the moment. Oftentimes, SJR becomes the connective tissue between the different units of corporations, sharing information about initiatives and different lines of business, and alerting stakeholders when the stories they request are duplicative of others' efforts.

To transfer knowledge externally, you have to first successfully transfer it internally, which is why we encourage our content teams to check in with other groups as often as possible. This way, your efforts are more all-encompassing, reaching corners of the organization where information and knowledge were previously buried, and ultimately none of your work is redundant or operationally inefficient—every marketing dollar is well spent.

It's one of the most gratifying parts of any SJR account, when our clients tell us that the content marketing function has become an essential tool for crossfunctional knowledge sharing, collaboration, and innovation.

With more collaboration, you're able to view your entire operation at a macro level. We like to think of it as an ecosystem (see Figure 8.1).

And while every person on your team has a different area of expertise and focus, content enables everyone to see how their piece fits in with the larger effort to transfer knowledge. All employees can

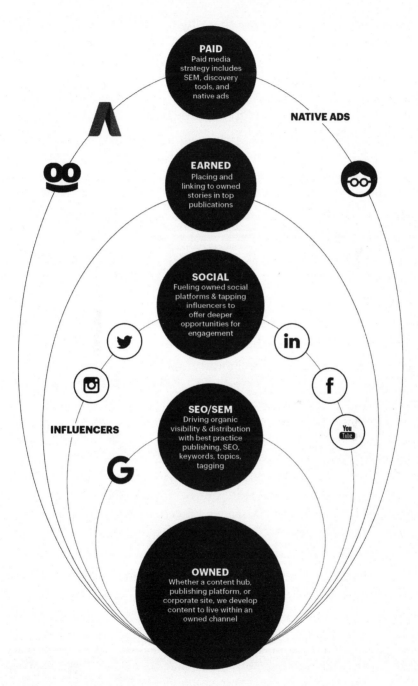

FIGURE 8.1 The Content Ecosystem.

feel a greater sense of purpose in their work and are held more accountable. It becomes a collective effort to set clear goals and establish reasons for everything the brand does—the pieces you're putting spend behind, what you're posting to Twitter versus what's going on Facebook, and the stories you're telling in the form of native advertisements as compared to those on your own content hub.

Sometimes, our clients are so eager to publish content that they forget about the entire ecosystem their content will live in. The enthusiasm is thrilling for us content marketers, but we often have to slow them down and get them to see the bigger picture. We help them gather all the different stakeholders from the outset and work with them to develop a plan for how every piece will fit together.

To transfer knowledge skillfully, collaboration is a necessity—this is as true for brands across departments as it is for agencies and publishers across the industry.

How the Industry Is Changing

Across the communications industry, there are seismic shifts happening. In marketing, PR, advertising, and strategic communications, we're seeing a convergence of agencies. Legacy advertising companies are coming to terms with the fact they don't have the in-house talent or expertise to do content marketing, and many newer, agile content marketing startups aren't scaled up to work with big brands yet. As a result, startups and large agencies need to work together to build our businesses and create our best work, thanks to a broader talent pool. It's a reality SJR has embraced, in our partnerships with some of our WPP sister companies: Ogilvy and Mather, Young and Rubicam, and J. Walter Thompson.

Outside of marketing, you see that the most successful businesses blend seamlessly with the competition. Apple uses Samsung processors in its iPhones.[1] Canon supplies photocopiers to Kodak.[2]

---

[1]Eric Zeman, "Samsung Supplying Apple's A9 Processor for Next iPhone," UBM, April 3, 2015, www.informationweek.com/mobile/mobile-devices/samsung-supplying-apples-a9-processor-for-next-iphone/a/d-id/1319766.
[2]Gary Hamel, Yvez Doz, and C. K. Prahalad, "Collaborate with Your Competitors—and Win," *Harvard Business Review*, January–February 1989, https://hbr.org/1989/01/collaborate-with-your-competitors-and-win.

Toyota and Suzuki have pooled their technological resources.[3] Our industry is no different, especially as content marketing enters an era of refinement and the expectation and investment for quality content is greater. Every agency, media company, and social platform has its own set of advantages—and to think any one company will reign supreme forever—is extremely foolish. At the end of the day, we work better together than separately, and in the future, I envision our work becoming even more fluid than it is now, especially with legacy media companies. You'll see traditional media companies, startups, publishers, video production companies, podcast creators, and other formerly disparate companies will mix and mingle. And just as SJR's work has improved through working with partners, I foresee content marketing as a whole will become more provocative, substantive, and collectively more profitable.

In our industry, big brands won't work with 10 to 20 different agencies in the future, especially as they build their own in-house teams (which are increasingly becoming more skilled at content marketing). They will seek to partner with the agencies with a proven track record across content, PR, media buying, social and so forth—with skills that complement those of their in-house team. And the only way for us to get better across the board is by leveraging each other's strengths. The takeaway? Don't be dismissive of any of your competitors or indirect competitors doing related work. Look for opportunities where you can work together. Hire people with a diversified skill set and an ability to teach others as well as a hunger to learn.

As our industry changes, our platforms are simultaneously evolving, becoming more ephemeral, visually driven, aesthetic, and user-centric, transforming how marketers communicate across them in the process.

Live content consumption is happening directly on social media platforms as opposed to in the past when sites like Facebook and Twitter merely referred links to users, taking them to a new website.

---

[3]Peter Lyon, "Toyota and Suzuki Announce Partnership, Leaving Japan's Auto-Industry Perplexed," *Forbes*, October 13, 2016, www.forbes.com/sites/peterlyon/2016/10/13/toyota-and-suzuki-announce-partnership-leaving-japans-auto-industry-perplexed/#9504a3827e74.

Today, on Twitter you can watch live sporting events. You can read articles authored by CEOs on LinkedIn rather than on the company blog or on *Forbes*. On Facebook, you can live stream events in 360 degrees. On Snapchat, brand influencers can privately send exclusive, personal videos and messages. As these platforms evolve to allow for more organic media consumption, you can view them as competitors to your hub, *or* you can work alongside them to form holistic communications strategies—where your strategy for each platform as compared to what you post on your website is distinct but fits collectively with your brand so your users will find new and exciting content on each channel. I promise you the latter option will work most to your benefit. You have to adapt along with these platforms, or you'll get left behind.

Beyond our work with other agencies, our thinking is that a direct relationship with social platforms and publishers is the strongest weapon we can have in our strategic arsenal.

As brands join new platforms—and I'm sure there will be many in the next few years—you need to get inside the heads of your users before you do anything. It's the only way you'll be able to make an impression. Building a solid team of out-of-the-box thinkers is the first step to achieving that, which we'll get to next.

Insights

- Collaboration and information sharing across your organization is the best way to create great content, reduce redundancies in communication, and ultimately create more operational efficiencies that can even save money.
- As content marketing matures, the industry faces growing pains. Agencies, publishers, social platforms, and startups are beginning to partner more on branded content. Stay open-minded and keep your ear to the ground for these opportunities—even legacy advertising agencies are realizing they need to invest more in content marketing.

Ask Yourself

- Is there enough cross-departmental communication? If not, how can it be improved?
- Are there any companies you'd want to partner with?
- If you're thinking about joining Snapchat or another live video service, what kinds of exclusive experiences will you give your fans? If you're already on it, how is your messaging resonating—what are people saying if they're snapping back or messaging?

9

Asymmetrical Thinking

W e are living in asymmetric times.

The threats and opportunities that will shape our future, even our immediate future, are likely to seem so small in the present that they are difficult to identify. Their importance now is not equal (or symmetrical) to their size later.

The cover of *The Economist*'s "World in 2017" issue, published in December of 2016, was a collage of all the world figures that the magazine's expert staff believed would shape the coming 12 months. Notably absent was the man who would win the U.S. presidential election and upend the world, Donald Trump. If I'd been designing the cover of that issue (and been able to see the future), I'd also have put the Twitter logo somewhere in the mix of recognizable faces.

Who would've guessed that a former reality TV star and a single social media platform would shape the destiny of hundreds of millions of people? What seemed at first absurd became unthinkable, then merely unlikely, then everybody's new reality.

A quote comes to mind from one of my favorite writers, Julio Cortazar: "Only by living absurdly is it possible to break out of this infinite absurdity."

Unless we learn to regularly sweep the horizon for threats and opportunities that are still small and refrain from dismissing them for seeming too weird or improbable, then we're likely doomed to be surprised by the future instead of prepared for it.

When I first heard of the concept of asymmetric warfare—the highly strategic way in which the military locates and prepares for unlikely threats that will grow larger over time—I realized how widely applicable the concept is in every aspect of life.

The Department of Defense's Joint Staff defines asymmetric warfare as "attempts to circumvent or undermine an opponent's strengths while exploiting his weaknesses *using methods that differ significantly from the opponent's usual mode of operation.*"[1]

In other words, an asymmetric warrior, or thinker, is not going head-to-head with his opponent in the traditional boots-on-the-ground sense. He or she gets creative and wins the war, solves the problem, or seizes the opportunity by resorting to unconventional approaches.

Asymmetric thinking challenges assumptions. I wouldn't call it thinking outside the box. When you think asymmetrically, you are free to ignore or rebuild the box entirely.

---

[1]Donald J. Wurzel, Kenneth R. McGruther, and William R. Murray, "A Survey of Unclassified Literature on the Subject of Asymmetric Warfare," (Sherman Oaks, CA: Arete Associates, 1998).

The concept has been around for thousands of years. In 500 B.C., Sun Tzu wrote, "If the enemy is superior in strength, evade him. If his forces are united, separate them. Attack him where he is unprepared."

"Appear where you are not expected."[2] We also see the concept play out in the ancient tale of the Trojan Horse from the *Iliad*, the epic poem that tells the story of the 10-year war between the citizens of Troy, a walled city, and the Greeks, camped outside the city and attempting to destroy it. After conventional warfare failed them, the Greeks resorted to asymmetrical warfare.

The Greeks, led by Odysseus, the ultimate asymmetric thinker, constructed a huge wooden horse that they gave to the Trojans as a gift—feigning surrender—and then pretended to sail away. We all know that the horse was a trap, concealing a few Greek warriors who emerged from the structure at night and unlocked the city gates, allowing the rest of their army, concealed nearby, to enter Troy and sack it. It wasn't strength that destroyed the Trojans but strategy and surprise.

Throughout history, countless military leaders have sought to leverage the same qualities, and in many cases, abiding by this venerable advice have led the dark horse, as it were, to succeed.

Guerilla warfare is one of the oldest forms of asymmetric warfare. Hebrew tribes used guerrilla tactics against Roman legions in the days before Christ. The Gauls and Celtic tribes also used guerrilla tactics, such as ambushes and deception, against the Romans during the Roman invasion and occupations of Germany and Britain. And the Germanic chieftain Arminius ambushed and destroyed three elite Roman legions in the Teutenburg Forest in 9 A.D.[3]

A more contemporary example is the 1,000-day Vietnam War, which proved to be the longest counter-guerrilla conflict fought by the U.S. military during the twentieth century. It was also the first time a technologically superior U.S. force was defeated, in a strategic sense, asymmetrically.

---

[2]Sun-tzu and Samuel B. Griffith, *The Art of War* (Oxford: Clarendon Press, 1964).
[3]Franklin B. Miles. "Asymmetric Warfare: A Historical Perspective." U.S. Army War College, March 17, 1999, 16. Accessed January 28, 2017.

Beyond war, pervasive asymmetrical challenges are present in every corner of our lives. Cybersecurity experts are threatened by hackers who are finding unprecedented and unforeseen ways to circumvent security systems experts had thought were nearly impenetrable. Hackers are the ultimate asymmetric fighters. They are able to take on enemies far larger than they are by turning a strength—the speed and interconnection that comes with the Internet—and turning it into a vulnerability. While it's possible for states of equal size to compete in cyberspace, the most ROI, so to speak, goes to the smaller ones fighting larger ones. A small collection of brilliant hackers anywhere can target the vital systems of any nation on earth, no matter how far away and no matter how much wealthier or more powerful.

Let's remove asymmetrical thinking from its military context and take a look at how it can be useful to strategic thinkers in business and in communications. The essence of asymmetric thinkers is that they aren't afraid to approach problems that seem much larger than their capabilities to address them. And they also take the unique attributes of each problem and do their best to turn them into advantages.

In the face of our most overwhelming difficulties, when the odds aren't in our favor, it's asymmetrical thinking that saves us. My favorite recent example of asymmetrical thinking is Paperfuge, a low-cost centrifuge invented by Manu Prakash, an assistant professor of bioengineering at Stanford University. The device costs only 20 cents to make, doesn't require electricity and can diagnose malaria, HIV, and other diseases—a groundbreaking invention for people in developing nations, who have little to no access to health care.[4]

Diagnostics in developed countries rely heavily on centrifuges, which are machines that can cost upwards of $1,000. They're essential to the process of using biological samples to diagnose disease.

How did Prakash come up with Paperfuge, which functions the same way a regular centrifuge does? He credits his upbringing in India, where he lacked access to tools he needed to do scientific research. He's also always had a fascination with toys, he told

[4]Ashley Strickland. "20-cent, whirligig-inspired Paperfuge could help diagnose diseases." January 16, 2017. Accessed January 28, 2017.

CNN, and thought he could replicate the speed of a yo-yo to create Paperfuge. For many months, he and his students analyzed all kinds of spinning toys, from tops to gyroscopes to whirligigs. Through a marathon of experiments and studies, the team was able to develop a human-powered centrifuge made of two synthetic polymer paper discs, braided fishing line, wood or PVC pipe for handles, drinking straws sealed with epoxy, and shatterproof plastic capillary tubes to hold the blood samples, according to CNN. The invention can separate pure plasma from blood in 90 seconds and isolate malaria parasites in just 15 minutes. The work also inspired a makeshift paper optical microscope he calls Foldscope that can be constructed for 50 cents and uses a piece of paper and a simple lens. He's in the process of testing both inventions in developing countries such as Madagascar with the goal of perfecting it for global distribution one day.

Determined to help democratize medicine, it was Prakash's asymmetrical approach—influenced by the fact that he never had a vast pool of resources growing up—that allowed him to invent such things. A few scraps of common supplies and some asymmetrical thinking might end up saving billions of dollars and countless lives.

Over the course of history, this is exactly how inventors who have few resources and a strong vision have operated. In the mid-1980s, British inventor Josh Silver developed low-cost eyeglasses in which the wearer can easily adjust the prescription, after a chance conversation with a colleague, according to *The Guardian*.[5] The glasses are unbelievably simple, relying on the basic principle that the thicker the lens is, the more powerful it becomes. Here's how his invention works: Inside the device's tough plastic lenses are two clear circular sacs filled with fluid, each of which is connected to a small syringe attached to either arm of the spectacles. The wearer adjusts a dial on the syringe to add or reduce the amount of fluid in the membrane, thereby changing the power of the lens. The implications of such a simple invention are huge. In developing nations, access to eye care is

---

[5]Esther Addley. "Inventor's 2020 vision: to help 1bn of the world's poorest see better," *The Guardian*, December 21, 2008, https://www.theguardian.com/society/2008/dec/22/diy-adjustable-glasses-josh-silver, accessed January 28, 2017.

almost a pipe dream—in sub-Saharan Africa the ratio of optometrists to people is 1:1,000,000. Allowing people in poor countries the ability to be their own optometrists will afford them the ability to learn to read, work more effectively (even retire later in life), take care of everyday tasks with ease, and ultimately live better lives.

Asymmetrical discovery and invention has been driving innovation for thousands of years. In the second century A.D., the Greek thinker Eratosthenes correctly deduced the circumference of the earth by measuring the angle of shadows cast by the sun at high noon in two places. Centuries later, European scientists using much more advanced tools confirmed that Eratosthenes was more or less right in his calculations, proof that no problem is too daunting when you make creative use of the tools at hand.

These are the stories we need to draw inspiration from in our nebulous line of work. Content marketing is relatively unchartered territory in the grand scheme of the communications and media industry. In each of our projects, it can feel like we're solving for X—aiming to conceptualize the best creative that will blow the competition out of the water and position our clients as thought leaders. We do this while operating with very limited resources and a series of hurdles, such as a small but talented staff, limited funding for big projects, or issues with different personalities and working styles that arise within our teams. The most important thing to remember is that we aren't *actually* solving for X. There is no X. There is no one right way of doing any of this, rather there is a realm of untapped possibilities that we need to constantly explore. In spite of the challenges—tight deadlines, a lack of budget, you name it—we've just got to figure it out by any means necessary.

At the companies I've co-founded, SJR, Truffle Pig, and Colloquial, our teams try to think asymmetrically all the time. In strategic communications, there are never ideal circumstances—you're constantly running into challenges—and the expectations are always very high. We are always called to do more with less—and most of the time, it enhances our creativity.

Asymmetric thinking is remarkably versatile. It can be applied to every challenge you face, big and small: finding new talent, pitching prospective clients, creating work that you can be proud of, growing the business, and creating new working methods.

Of the many challenges we encounter, the most important is having the right talent on board. Because at the end of the day, your strategies are born from *people*.

We have a tendency to group people into buckets. It's human instinct. We assess people based on what they've done rather than considering the vast untapped potential of what they can do. But how can you grow unless you let your people grow?

Especially if you're aiming to create truly original content that's going to drive clients' business outcomes—the kind of work that gets you contract renewals year after year and makes you an indispensable part of brands' marketing efforts.

At SJR, Truffle Pig, Colloquial, and Hill+Knowlton Strategies, hiring asymmetrically for us means hiring generalists not specialists. Unlike other consulting firms and many other agencies that have practice areas, we want our teams to have (or develop) truly eclectic skill sets and backgrounds so they bring fresh thinking to content programs. We're building teams that flourish in our asymmetric world, which demands velocity and novel approaches to the most complicated problems.

So we'll hire fine artists who might not have ever done commercial work before and part-time poets to infuse our new business pitches with truly original thinking. We'll have our engineers work in illustration and our account leads double as producers on set.

We do this because our people are more than their titles. Truth be told, I would do away with titles altogether if I could. Because titles are reductionist and never capture the incredible range of abilities that our people have. Our best work comes from the people you'd least expect it from. And we'll continue to encourage our people to tinker and explore new accounts and ways of doing things. It's better for our people, and it's better for our business—it is this approach that allows us to win contracts away from agencies 20 times our size and to see threats and opportunities while they are still on the horizon.

At SJR, we call our most versatile talent "zebra talent" for two reasons. The first is that they have stripes and aren't just limited to one color. In other words, they can do more than one kind of job. The second reason is that we believe there are no unicorns, no perfect fits for the job openings you have. There are only zebras, people who will surprise you with the many things they can do, if you are open to the possibilities.

Insights

+ No problem is too big to be solved by a creative, asymmetric use of whatever tools are at hand.
+ When deciding who will work on a client project, give others a chance to contribute. Often, it's the people you'd least expect who are able to give the most. And it's often the people who aren't extremely familiar with the subject matter—the outsiders—who are able to come up with novel solutions and ideas.

Ask Yourself

+ What are some ways that your team has thought asymmetrically? How could they integrate this kind of thinking into your work each day?
+ When you look at all the people on your team, have you hired a group of problem-solvers focused on coming up with solutions even in unfavorable circumstances?
+ How will you inspire your team to think asymmetrically?

Afterword: The Future of Storytelling

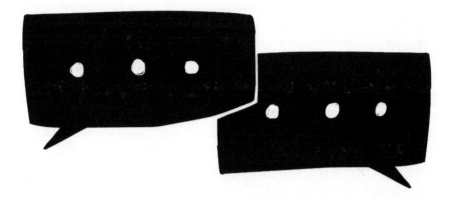

Asymmetrical thinking teaches us that the seeds of the future are contained in the present. We just have to train ourselves to see them and have the imagination to believe that they will grow into forces and trends fully capable of reshaping our world.

Storytelling, as much as any other activity, is subject to asymmetric disruption and growth. The small-scale, low-status content of the past inevitably rises to prominence in the future.

Before becoming court entertainment for English royalty, Shakespeare's plays were seen as sensational, corrupting content fit only for the lowest status members of society. As a form, novels began their cultural life as a guilty pleasure, printed by the chapter in the back pages of newspapers. In the 1940s and 1950s, comic books had a status little higher than pornography in the U.S. media landscape, and were attacked as a corrupting influence on the children who read them. Yet in the second decade of the twenty-first century, Marvel's Avengers franchise, based on classic comic book characters, has produced some of the highest-grossing films of all time and has been purchased by the ultimate mainstream global media company, Walt Disney.

If we look at today's media landscape, there are a number of trends and innovations which, though seen as edge cases today, will likely grow or rise in status in the future, becoming as respected and ubiquitous as any form that came before.

First on the list is content marketing. Despite its pervasiveness, branded content is still fenced off into a category all its own, kept separate from either journalism or mainstream entertainment. In the future, I believe the borders that separate branded from unbranded content will become less relevant in some cases or will be simply ignored or invisible in others. Branded content never need replace the breaking news and opinion sections of respected outlets like the *New York Times* or the daily news programming on the major networks, but it is primed to become equal in status with specialty magazines like *Wired* or *Fast Company*, or lifestyle publications like *Women's Health* or *Outside*. There's also nothing preventing major brands from sponsoring high-end programming in the infotainment space—shows like 2014's *Cosmos* with Neil deGrasse Tyson, or the BBC's blockbuster nature documentary *Planet Earth*.

Next up is storytelling assisted by artificial intelligence. AI is already an $8 billion market, set to grow to $47 billion by 2020. It is transforming retail, health care, heavy industry, scientific research, and conservation. And it is beginning to transform storytelling as well. Some creative agencies in the United States and Japan are starting to execute on creative briefs generated by AI, which have processed reams of customer and demographic data, determining precisely which messages will help a product or idea resonate the most with an intended group. This process is a novelty at the moment, but will no doubt become standard practice in the future. We'll always need human creatives, but there's no reason they should shy away from collaborating with nonhuman minds.

Personalization is another trend set to transform the way stories are told. The more data we choose to share about ourselves, the more the systems we rely on are primed to identify and even anticipate our needs. The holy grail of storytelling for any master brand is an extended story that evolves and deepens every time a customer interacts with a brand, in just such a way that the customer is surprised, delighted, and satisfied.

Until now, brands have had to rely on a single guiding narrative to design customer interactions around, and then hope for the best. In the era of radical personalization, consumers might have something like their own master narrative, offered in atomized form across their devices and interactions, refined across the span of their entire life. This, combined with trends in augmented reality, gamification, and so-called blended reality, in which digital information is overlaid into a consumer's real-world visual and tactile environment, could combine into the first truly immersive forms of storytelling. Personalization in this context could produce content that creates a dynamic, deepening relationship between a consumer and a brand, where both change over time.

These new forms of storytelling will not stay put in our lives, consigned only to feed us information. They will inevitably help us do other things as well. I've already spoken about the ability of stories to transform the companies that tell them. In the future, any consultancy or innovation practice will be incomplete unless it has a capacity to tell stories, about itself, its clients, and the world. And just as highly customized, insightful stories are helping organizations make decisions, there is no reason the same might not be true of our personal stories, made richer and more complete by access to our own reservoir of personal data. We humans have always told stories about our lives to help us make sense of what to do next, and in the future our technology will give us tools to make those stories even better. In addition to our journals, our memories, and our friends, we will also have our data and new ways to understand it.

What I've given here is a sketch of future storytelling suggested by new technology emerging as of this writing. But even by the time this book is in print, there will be other forms, more powerful and stranger than what I've laid out here. There always will be. When it comes to the inventiveness of the human imagination, the continuous emergence of the new is the only constant.

One of the few hard and fast rules of media history is that no form has risen to newfound dominance at the expense of all the past ones. New media always coexists with its predecessors. Just as there are still groups of people skilled at making stone tools, there are groups skilled in the art of oral storytelling and epic poetry, memorized and recited or sung live. These forms are no longer part of our daily lives, but they have not died out nor are they likely to. And we still have books, newspapers, plays, movies, comics, video games, and all the other forms of storytelling that human culture has developed over the ages. Our appetite for new stories always grows, never diminishes.

What this means for brands and storytellers is that there will always be new formats to explore and old ones to master. Your ability to tell stories and the interest of your customers and the public in consuming them are inexhaustible.

To some, this constant change is cause for anxiety. But to me and to anyone reading this book (I hope), it is unequivocally good news. As I said in the opening pages, we will always need more storytellers than we currently have.

If you've been helped or inspired by what you've read here, and especially if you've been moved to tell your own story based on what you've read, I'd love to hear more.

Fondly,
Alexander Jutkowitz
thestrategicstoryteller@groupsjr.com
alexanderjutkowitz.com

Index